HIGHWAY TO
HISTORY

A CYCLING ADVENTURE ON ROUTE 66

DAVID FREEZE

Published by:
Walnut Creek Farm Publishing
China Grove, N.C. 28023

Designed by Andy Mooney
Map illustration by Andy Mooney
Cover photography by Jon C. Lakey

ISBN 978-0-692-79991-8

On the front: Classic cars were a common sight along Route 66, such as the beautifully restored 1955 Chevrolet Bel Air, owned by Jake Speck of Salisbury, N.C. **On the back:** David and Jake chat in front of the Dairy Queen in Salisbury, owned by Melissa Utley.

FOREWORD

"Even if you're on the right track, you'll get run over if you just sit there," Will Rogers once said.

No one would accuse David Freeze of just sitting there. David found his "right track" — solo, cross-country cycling adventures — in the summer of 2013, when he pedaled from Oregon to South Carolina. He's been mapping out routes ever since, taking in new sights and meeting countless people on his summer journeys.

In June 2016, David set out on Route 66, also dubbed the Will Rogers Highway, in part because one of the states it crosses is Rogers' home state of Oklahoma. The route is also known for the 1960s TV show, "Route 66," a drama centered on two handsome and enviously footloose young men seeking adventure. They were the epitome of cool.

A popular record of that era, "Get Your Kicks on Route 66," cinched the image. If the '60s were the height of America's love affair with the automobile, charging down Route 66 in a svelte Corvette with no particular destination in mind, well, that was the ultimate fantasy.

Route 66 was historic before TV was born. It was the Mother Road, a main artery extending from Chicago to California that carried people through the Dustbowl, the Depression and countless family vacations.

I say this by way of explaining the gush of remembrance and joy expressed toward David when he returned to his North Carolina hometown at the end of his 2016 journey. The Salisbury Post had published his daily chronicles of the trip, as we have done each year, and we invited readers to welcome him home at a reception in our lobby. They had gotten their kicks following David on Route 66, and they were eager to thank him for it.

An adage often cited in the Post's newsroom is, "All roads lead to Salisbury"— meaning nearly every major news event has a Salisbury connection. At the reception, it seemed all lives led to Route 66. Everyone had a connection or a favorite spot, and they were as eager to share their stories as they were to hear David's.

David says he starts thinking about his next trip before he finishes the one he's on. His fans seem to do the same thing, as more than one person at the reception offered suggestions for his 2017 trip. After four summers of following his travels, they had little doubt David would do it again.

It will be hard to top Route 66, though.

The historic highway is a throwback to the simpler days of family travel, when long routes were dotted with unique attractions — like a line of ancient Cadillacs buried nose first in the desert — and roadside inns and restaurants were as varied as the characters who ran them.

You'll meet some of those characters — and see the Cadillacs — as you read this book. As always, my hat's off to David for enduring a rigorous journey and meeting deadline every night. What a gift his stories are to loyal readers. What a joy it is to tap his spirit of adventure.

Let's end with another wise observation from Will Rogers.

"If you want to be successful, it's just this simple. Know what you are doing. Love what you are doing. And believe in what you are doing."

David believes — and so do we.

— **Elizabeth Cook**
Editor, Salisbury Post

ACKNOWLEDGMENTS

More than ever before, I realize that I have the easiest responsibility when it comes to another book. I get to go ride the bike and see America for weeks at a time. When I return home, the real work begins. Just as with the previous books, the real professionals take over and turn out a first class publication. While it is important to me to do this right, I would be lost without the following folks who bring the book to life.

Once again, Salisbury Post Editor Elizabeth Cook has contributed the foreword. She is also one of my biggest cheerleaders during the pre- and post-trip details. News Editor Scott Jenkins took over as the lead editor for the book and did a great job. Photographer Jon C. Lakey keeps coming up with ways to make me look good. Creative Director Andy Mooney pulls all of the material together with his own editing, graphics and layout skills. The credit for the quality of Highway to History goes entirely to this fine group of friends and professionals. I learn more from them each time we work together.

My friends and family back home kept the farm and home responsibilities going. Special thanks again to Mrs. Ollie McKnight and farm manager Sam Freeze, along with my daughters, Ashley Baker and Amber Freeze, for their work as I pedaled away.

Friends who made contributions and supported the trip include Dr. Delaine Fowler, Dr. Tanya Williams, Eric Phillips, Luis Villareal, Peter Asciutto, Leonard Wood, Tim and Linda Hoffner and First Baptist Church of China Grove. The Salisbury Post remains the catalyst for each one of my journeys and certainly there would be a huge void had we not kicked off an uncertain coast to coast ride together in 2013.

And, more than ever, those readers who chimed in with sugges-tions about places to go and what to see greatly helped me with my daily planning as the ride developed. Still others offered prayers and encouragement that was appreciated more than I can express. With the presence of God and the many readers who were invested in my Route 66 ride, I certainly never felt alone. I am continually humbled by the appeal of these adventures. Thank you!

INTRODUCTION

With certainty, once the previous cycling adventure has been completed, the time has lessened before I am ready to saddle up again. Could it be that I have become addicted to the authentic adventures of solo endurance bicycle riding across America? From just a three-day journey in the West Virginia wilderness came the quest for the new and sometimes unimagined that has nourished itself into almost an obsession to experience more of the greatest country on earth.

Until just a few short years ago, I had no inkling that any sport other than competitive running would garner my central focus. Now with more than 4,000 miles from Oregon to South Carolina, and almost 3,000 each on trips from Maine to Key West and from Alabama to Canada, I have become a veteran of "touring" — long and unsupported excursions on bicycle.

My thoughts have run the gamut from apprehension with the first ride to almost an obsession now to complete cycling journeys that include as many states as possible. I love reading and watching sports and news on TV, especially now that the far-reaching points of this great nation seem so much closer. But much more than that, my adventures occur at a pace where I can readily absorb the scenery and the people, soaking up their heritage and traditions.

While in search of adventures that others have thought of but few have attempted, I have relished the experiences of flying in a B-17 bomber and a Pitts Special aerobatic plane. Skydiving and flying a glider were amazing, too. I have been fortunate to win numerous awards in running competitions. But all of these are fleeting memories. As of yet, nothing matches the ongoing excitement of riding the backroads through the welcoming communities to experience again the inherent goodness of their inhabitants. Add in the incredible scenery and my dreams are fulfilled.

Such was the vision of yet another dream as I considered options for the summer 2016 ride. Once Route 66 became the next possible thread in the tapestry of my bike routes across America, excitement and momentum built quickly. America's most legendary highway tempted me as I gathered knowledge from multiple sources. There were enough historical details, always a required part of my cycling, to make me search for more.

The old road, at least a major part of it, is something like an aging celebrity who has experienced a major comeback. The attempts of five interstates have failed to take its place and cannot begin to match the amazing personality of a road that has reached iconic status. I dare to exit the highway on the bike and look for the hidden and forgotten, the good old days, the nostalgia and the romance.

So, now it's time to settle back and ride with me once again as we pack up the bike and head out for another entry in my serious love affair with roadside America. I don't want to miss a thing. Come ride along, from Santa Monica to Chicago and beyond, as we discover why Route 66 remains active and relevant to this day.

CHAPTER ①

Getting it together for another cycling adventure

Yes, it's time for another long ride. The thoughts of another cycling adventure have not been too far from my mind since I pedaled into Toronto last year. A few followers expected this of me, but even my closest friends and family knew little about the details except that I wanted to ride the length of Route 66 from California to Chicago. There certainly would be a few side trips, but the focus was the "Mother Road," the superhighway of its day that opened the way to the West Coast from Chicago.

My goal was to have pedaled through about 40 states by the time this Route 66 ride was over. The previous adventures included a short, three-day ride through the Greenbrier section of West Virginia before the more serious and involved endurance efforts of the next three summers. My cross-country ride happened in the summer of 2013, when I ventured out to Astoria, Oregon, to ride 4,164 miles all the way back through North Carolina and then on to Myrtle Beach, South Carolina, to finish up the coast-to-coast experience. The biggest part of the route followed what is called the Transamerica Trail, although I did break off from it to pass by my own farm before heading to Myrtle Beach.

With the wonderful experience of the cross-country ride in the rearview mirror, I was certainly hooked and ready to get on the road again. After much thought, I chose the more heavily populated East Coast route from the easternmost point in the U.S. to the southernmost point. We later referred to this one as the Maine to Key West adventure. The ride included battling more traffic than I had seen previously and, eventually, a serious collision with a car. The coast was filled with beautiful scenery, plenty of history and more of the wonderful people I had come to expect along the way.

With two of these big rides done, I had to get another one going. The next ride was full of history after I chose one of the principal routes of the Underground Railroad. Being a huge history buff, I thought it would be exciting to ride through some of the venues and routes that the escaped slaves followed to venture north all the way to Canada and their longed-for freedom. Mobile, Alabama, was the starting point, with the Underground Railroad terminus coming at Owen Sound, Ontario. Some bonus riding finished off the experience when I rode two days east into Toronto from Owen Sound.

My thoughts during those final days were already on where I could go next to get more of the same kinds of experiences and add more states as yet new to my bicycle. A small group of new states was in the Northwest and another was in the Southwest. After buying the Adventure Cycling maps of both areas, my choice actually flip-flopped back and forth a few times. While taking plenty of time to analyze the length and climbing challenges of the two routes and matching up with my available time frame for travel, my first thought was to take the Northwest route that is often called part of the Northern Tier in cycling circles. Although neither route was exceptionally harder physically than the other, the extreme temperatures of the desert in summer added a big concern. Yet, the more I read about Route 66 and its journey through the desert Southwest, the more I was intrigued by it.

If the choice did become Route 66, I could add California, Arizona, New Mexico and Oklahoma as new states and at least be able to consider side trips to Nebraska and Michigan. A northern route would add Washington, North and South Dakota, Minnesota, Wisconsin and there was the opportunity to add Iowa. With about six weeks to go, I decided to go to the desert and planned to leave about two weeks earlier than the previous summer. My flight was set for June 14, with Santa Monica, California, slated as the starting point on June 15.

With the airline ticket secured, I set about finding a bike shop to reassemble my Surly Long Haul Trucker after it was shipped from Salisbury. I called Cynergy Cycles in Santa Monica, and after a series of purposeful conversations with them, I had Skinny Wheels Bike Shop package and ship the bike west. The last piece remaining was to secure a motel room for that first night. I inquired as to the possibilities and found all of the usually reasonable choices much more expensive on the California coast. Nothing seemed to be the proper fit, and thus began my first experience with Airbnb. Learning as I went, I eventually found what seemed like the best alternative to a motel room just a few blocks from Cynergy Cycles and still near the beach and reasonable food choices. Booking the Airbnb location was easy, and I was set to begin my newest adventure.

Airbnb served as my option to rent part of a home or a private apartment instead of a motel or hotel room. Private owners had listed their properties with the amenities included and price on the Airbnb site, and I was encouraged to use it by the guys at the Cynergy Cycles. Booking a private residence was billed as a chance to really live the life of a resident, and I was intrigued by it. My separate apartment was booked with Vasil, a Santa Monica chiropractor, with his promise to meet me upon arrival.

No major changes were planned with my bike and gear. The same Surly Long Haul Trucker was my vehicle for the Underground Railroad and did very well. The same Brooks B17 seat was a holdover from all three previous rides and so was much of the gear that would fill my panniers. The same light sleeping bag, half-body air mattress and tent were all proven and ready to go. Basic clothing and supplies were the same, as was the tool kit. I had the same bicycle helmet, too, although I had considered a change for comfort. My light and breathable rain coat would go along again, although I expected that any rain in the first two to three weeks would feel very good.

Lesser changes from previous rides included just three things. I had a wide-brimmed cloth hat, purchased from Dick's Sporting Goods right before I left, to shield against the expected brilliant desert sun and extreme temperatures. Another new item was suggested by Claire Watts, a neighbor and running friend. Claire told me about roll-up water bottles that would take less space when not in use. I bought three of the large, one-liter bottles and packed them easily.

Last came a different approach to how I would use a manual pump/CO2 cartridge combination to fill my tire tubes with air as the trip developed. Previously, most of my tire filling came from using those two together, even though my newest pump was not good at connecting with the crossover valve that allowed use of a commercial air hose or a CO2 cartridge. I decided to take the pump as only a last resort and planned to make extensive use of the CO2 cartridges.

With all these things covered, I wanted to do two more things in the last two weeks before beginning the journey. The first was the simplest and yet the most important. Following the completion of all three of my long rides, I have had serious medical issues with blood clots. Although I don't have properties in my blood that cause extra or unique clotting, the cross-country ride resulted in an extreme DVT in the weeks following my ride. Further complications included multiple clots in my lungs and a brain tumor found when checking my brain for clots.

A DVT is a deep vein thrombosis, a large blood clot that impedes blood flow to the rest of the body. Serious complications happen when small pieces of the clot break off and eventually clog a major artery and stop blood flow completely. That process is called a pulmonary embolism and is often deadly. After the DVT formed near the end of my cross-country ride, the pieces that traveled from the major clot in my leg thankfully made it to my lungs without any catastrophic result. My lungs were described as full of clots, and that fact caused doctors to check my brain.

While some might support a problem with a non-medical problem with my brain, two resulting MRIs found no clots but that I did have a small brain tumor that appeared non-malignant. A renowned brain surgeon in Charlotte suggested a wait of six months to get me off the blood thinner and to monitor the growth of the tumor. A second opinion called for another MRI about two months after the discovery of the tumor. That MRI found that the tumor was no longer in my brain but doctors had no real explanation for how this occurred. I could only credit continual prayer from myself and so many others for the unexpected miracle.

Symptoms of the clots that tipped me off to the 2013 problem were issues with breathing, a rapid resting pulse, inability to exercise at a strenuous level and, finally, pain below the DVT location in the leg. I did not think that I had the clotting while riding. The strenuous uphill rides through the Rockies and Ozarks would not have been possible under the breathing limitations. Use of a blood thinner improved the symptoms in a matter of days, and the DVT cleared within several months.

At the end of the 2014 East Coast ride — in fact, just a few days after the accident with the automobile in Florida — my feet began to swell, and the clotting issue was back. After much discussion and thought with the local Salisbury, I was sent to the Vascular Department at Wake Forest Baptist Medical Center in Winston-Salem. Months on blood thinner cleared up the issue once again.

I felt great heading into the Underground Railroad ride of 2015 and frankly expected that all of these clot issues were in the past. Lucky and decent in more than a few sports, my confidence assured me that I could resume this intense activity without any limitations. A week after arriving home after the completion of this journey, I was so confident that I told others that there was not a clotting issue this time. Just a few days later, however, my breathing and resting pulse both were working very hard after just a minimum of activity. Thoughts began to creep into my mind that I had developed yet another DVT.

In fact, the clot was back, and it was a big one. The local doctors thought that I had one that was susceptible to moving while still large, thus capable of causing real problems. Back to Baptist and the Vascular Department I went, even though somehow I missed that the patient should not be driving himself. Dr. Levy, head of the department, expressed real concern about the recurring DVTs and told me, "You know, this is the place where I should tell you that you can't do this anymore."

So after the blood thinner did some more good work, I was clear again but not totally free to head for another long ride, this one involving some elevation and extremely hot and sustained temperatures. Both of these factors were thought to have played a part in the 2013 cross-country ride clot, my first one ever. Dr. Levy asked me to make sure I took a baby aspirin each day, stayed hydrated and resumed the blood thinner even a couple of days before the ride was completed. The reason that I could not continue on the blood thinner during the time on the bike was that any accident could cause severe bleeding that would be almost impossible to stop, particularly in the remote areas where much of the riding would occur.

The other thing I wanted to do before heading for California was to read as much as I could about Route 66. I got a series of books from Jerry McClanahan, a longtime expert on the subject, and read all three from cover to cover. There were several YouTube videos on Route 66 worth watching, including one that was supposed to be a sped up helmet camera view of all the roads along the way.

By this time, I had seen, read and heard about so many interesting sites that I wanted to include all of them that I could in my ride along the Mother Road. Traveling on a bike was somewhat limiting at times, because ten miles off the route was a long way on a bike and a long way back. Therefore, I wanted to be prepared to see all the things on my list. Right away, I also realized that there were multiple Route 66 alignments out there, some not used since 1940. Others were even earlier, only driven in the 1920s.

While every ounce of weight matters on a solo touring bike, it did not take me long to realize that I would have to carry at least one of the route guides. I chose the one that seemed best to me and also took my Adventure Cycling Route 66 maps. I planned to buy individual state maps along the way.

With only a limited knowledge of "Grapes of Wrath" by John Steinbeck and the song, "Get Your Kicks on Route 66" by Bobby Troup, I barely remembered the TV series, "Route 66". A few "Route 66" reruns still popular on some of the nostalgia channels were worth watching. It was time to go for another long ride, one that excited me just a little more each day.

In the 1950s and '60s, many of the original Route 66 roadways were replaced by a system of interstate highways. I knew in advance that some parts of Route 66 were no longer there at all, others were impassable, and still others had been given other road names. Yet, the spirit of the great Mother Road remained, and I was going to see it up close from a bicycle seat. I couldn't wait!

CHAPTER ②

As always, my last week at home was filled with plenty of list making and hustling around trying to check off those things that can put my daily life back in North Carolina on the slow burner for about six weeks. With each hour that passes, more gets done and the more my thoughts propel me toward the beginning of the next adventure. Such was the case this time, and few real worries were on my mind.

One issue that intrigued me was how to handle the extreme heat. I had been plenty hot before on one of these rides, specifically four straight 100-degree days in the plains of Kansas during 2013's cross-country ride. This time, the temperature could be as much as 15-20 degrees hotter. Other issues seemed minimal, while this heat demanded a broader stage as the ride drew near. More than one person asked me to consider delaying the departure until a cooler time, which absolutely was not an option.

On Tuesday, June 14, my daughter Amber picked me up at the farm for the ride to the airport. Just before the start of previous rides, there have typically been a couple of times that doubt would creep in just before the actual ride began. One was often on the morning that we headed to the airport, usually just about the time that Amber or someone drops me off. Although I remember the final goodbye as a time of previous doubt, this time it didn't happen. I don't take much baggage with me because anything must fit in my panniers, so I stood there holding only a backpack. We stayed for a long time just outside the airport doors and hugged, knowing that at best it would be about six weeks before we would see each other again.

I went inside, easily got my ticket and quickly passed through security. Maybe it is just my own impression, but the process always seems to go better on the way out of Charlotte or Greensboro than some of the bigger airports. Inside the airport shortly afterwards with just my thoughts, I found a rocker to sit in and watch the dawn sky gradually brighten while looking over my maps and Route 66 information.

Slowly, the time arrived when I needed to head for my gate. Right away, the airline announced that the plane was full and added all the usual following statements. When my zone was finally called and we headed for the plane, it was time for the second round of doubt to sneak in if it had an opening. I remembered boarding the plane before heading to Maine a couple of years ago and wondering if I was ready for this. There was some concern about the high-traffic areas and the fact that both of my first two days each needed to total over 100 miles ridden. There was none of that this time; I was ready to go and get the show on the road.

Both connecting flights seemed long, and although I had some good conversation on the Cincinnati to Los Angeles portion of it, sitting that long had me restless and ready to get out of those seats. The second flight was delayed in landing at Los Angeles, and it was about all I could stand to keep sitting any longer. But I knew at this point that a "whole new adventure" was about to begin, most likely just minutes away.

Not being an Uber person yet, I was told that the best way to get to the bike shop probably was a cab. I had read about the cost of a cab ride to the beach and asked — although I was a little worried that few people were taking them — where to find one. Lots of traffic, including shuttles but very few cabs for such a big airport, was almost paralyzing the streets. Still, I found one and what resulted was a $50 cab ride that covered about ten miles, including where the driver didn't see Cynergy Cycles and had to double back with the meter running. I saw it as a sign of trouble when the driver could not get my debit card to work, but finally I was off a plane, out of a cab and in the palm trees and streets of Santa Monica, California.

My previous conversations with Cynergy Cycles had been good, and the store looked fantastic from outside. However, during my cycling travels, I have repeatedly learned that once the door is opened, the real demeanor of a bike shop will soon show itself. Diego at Cynergy had told me that their policy was not to open a bike box until the owner was present so that he could see how the package arrived and with what damage. I had asked him to waive this policy so that I could get the bike as quickly as possible upon arrival.

The professionalism of the crew at Cynergy Cycles was apparent at every turn once I entered the store. I told them who I was — they were expecting me, of course — and within minutes they brought my bike around the corner. The bike was totally clean, put together perfectly, and my additional gear was right there, too. Diego told me that the box had arrived banged up a little, that not enough packing was used and there was some scratching on the frame. He had videoed the process of taking the bike out of the box.

Regardless, I was pleased with the way the bike looked and took some time to put my gear in the panniers right away. I bought a couple of tubes and CO_2 cartridges and realized that I needed two new water bottles. They gave me the bottles and I paid for the other stuff, just before giving them one of my books and heading out the door to find my Airbnb apartment. Job well done, Cynergy Cycles!

Traffic was moderately heavy, but I still got on the bike and headed down the street and toward the address that I had. My host for the evening had listed a small, separate apartment for me to use on this one night in Santa Monica. Vasil was in the yard, expecting me, and right away made me feel welcome and offered a quick tour. The tour showed that I had my own room and bathroom, as well as an entrance that would keep me from disturbing anyone.

Vasil raced motorcycles and had a bicycle or two on the walls. He offered his tools before telling me that he worked most afternoons and early evenings. I declined on the tools, thinking I had what I needed, and listened as he told me what was in the area. After all that sitting, I desperately wanted to walk down to the beach and the famous Santa Monica Pier. I left my bike in the garage and a few possessions in the room as I headed for the beach on a cool and almost perfect afternoon. As I remember, the temperature was in the mid- to upper-70s, just as perfect as several friends who had visited the area previously suggested that it would be.

The early start and the westward travel kept six hours of flying and all the extra time parking and moving about the airports in a tight package that left me enough time to experience a long afternoon in the area. Santa Monica, at least to a longtime country boy, was beautiful and interesting at every corner. There were lots of shops, plenty of apartments for rent or for sale, and wide open sidewalks and streets. It was about a ten-block walk to the beach, and my legs felt good to be working again, especially knowing that beginning early the next morning, I would not be doing much walking.

Encounters with the locals on the sidewalk were all friendly, and I realized immediately that walking and cycling were both extremely popular for the Santa Monica residents. About 3 p.m., I made it to the bluff overlooking the Pacific and began walking toward the pier in the distance. It was a hazy and overcast day, making me wonder if my hoped-for Pacific sunset would happen. Anytime I am near the Pacific Ocean or a westward-looking, large body of water, I anticipate the sight of the sun settling so serenely into the water. Recalling the Key West and Lake Erie sunsets of the last two summers brought to mind an almost a magical experience.

On this day, the beach was crowded and even more so was the pier area. Popularly considered the symbolic end/start of Route 66, the Santa Monica Pier, originally constructed in 1908, included lots of shops, restaurants and rides. The pier area included a nine-story Ferris wheel and a five-story roller coaster. The carousel on the pier is a 1922 model, featured prominently in the 1973 movie "The Sting," with Paul Newman and Robert Redford.

A marker was dedicated in 2009 designating the pier as the end/start of Route 66. It was also the first time that I saw the soon-to-be-commonplace Route 66 Highway shields painted on the roads. Later, each state would keep the same basic design but include their state names in the background. Originally, the official terminus of Route 66 followed Santa Monica Boulevard, then took a left on Lincoln Boulevard before ending at Olympic.

Being a people watcher, I alternately walked and watched the people while observing more than one oddity. I walked through Pacific Palisades Park, one of those beautiful-sounding names that I will add to along the next 2,500 miles. I saw street performers, some extremely good and all hoping to draw the spectators in closer.

As the afternoon's hazy shadows drew longer, I headed back toward my apartment and got some food, including a Subway sandwich that was the same price and almost as good as those near home. The neighborhood grocery was awesome and had just reduced in price their baked goods, which was perfect timing for me. Pastries and bread go a long way toward fueling my bike rides and there were no limits on eating them during these adventures.

Later, I walked back to the beach and realized that there would be no sunset seen on this day, so I returned to the apartment and made sure that all was ready for my departure east early the next morning. The first part of the riding was going to be on the busy city streets of the Los Angeles suburbs, and I wanted my bike ready to go. A good night's sleep was on my mind, even though I was still not tired regardless of the time difference between the East Coast and West Coast.

Usually as I head for bed on the last night before the ride begins, I briefly look back over any concerns just briefly and think about all the things that I have learned that will make this trip better. The only concern remaining at this point was to make sure to heed all the precautions to stay hydrated during the quickly upcoming extreme heat. But just like always, I had no trouble giving the worry over to God and letting Him handle it. That was just what I did on this night and very quickly was sound asleep.

During the night, I heard someone briefly knocking on the door and was surprised to find that it was Vasil's dog. I told him to stop and he did, never to be heard from again. My two extra hours of sleep still got me packed and out on the street just as daylight was coming, also a regular occurrence for the rest of the ride.

The ride began. My first tenths clicked off as I rode down to the beach and pier for a few photos before heading east. Just about a mile was enough to reach the ocean, and I looked around on the pier with almost no one present. Good photos in the early morning remained my favorite, and a few presented themselves. I got a picture of the Forrest Gump bench at the Bubba Gump Shrimp Company. I read Forrest's line printed on the bench, "Life is like a box of chocolates …" and then walked the bike down a steep stairway to the beach while I thought about the rest of Gump's statement. He said, "You never know what you are going to get." This statement certainly fit my upcoming ride, because like all of them, I didn't really know what I was going to get over the upcoming days.

A cool plaque called Santa Monica "Muscle Beach," and I got a photo of that, too. Only one person was in sight, but my experience with trying to take a wheel-dipping photo myself had gone so badly in the past, I still thought it best to bother him as he sat on a bench looking at the ocean.

Just as I expected, the man was surprised that anyone would want to take a photo of his back wheel getting wet in the ocean. Still, without getting too close or saying too much, the man was nice enough to take a few photos and congratulate me on the ride that was ahead, although he had a hard time comprehending how long it would take. As soon as he handed my iPad back, the man disappeared. I took a few more looks around, thought about the next six weeks and said a few more prayers. I climbed back up off the beach and back onto Ocean Boulevard. After walking the bike some more, I climbed on and headed east on Broadway. Yes, the ride was now officially on. "Lord, ride with me!"

The extra sleep and maybe some of the first day excitement made me feel strong on this first day. What stretched out ahead seemed so huge as the single miles slowly started to pile up. The bike guys at Cynergy Cycles had warned me about the harried drivers on the Santa Monica and LA streets early in the day. I did not have any trouble with them, but I sure did get tired of stopping at the hundreds of red lights while it was easy to cheer during the few that stayed green for a quick ride through. Nobody blew a horn at me although there were not many bike lanes where I could separate from traffic.

A few drops of misty rain fell, but the clouds probably had more to do with smog than anything else. The temperature remained perfect for riding, no matter what. I started to check off the LA suburbs, and Beverly Hills was first. I had always thought of Beverly Hills as a very exclusive area where expensive cars and shops would dominate the scenery, I found Beverly Hills to be just about that but still friendly enough. My guidebook said that Beverly Hills remained synonymous with movie stars and other rich types. A common happening in the area was to buy a map of the homes of the movie stars and go look for them, but I heard that an even better tactic was to inquire where filming was being done and go there. The Sharon Tate murders happened here in 1969, and gangster Bugsy Siegel was gunned down in 1947. Marilyn Monroe and Natalie Wood were buried close by.

My maps directed me through a residential area of very fine homes and four-way stops that were endless. Because it took so long to completely stop and hop down off a bike, I was tempted to just keep riding if no one was around. I had made a pledge to myself to follow as many of the road and street laws as possible, so I kept on slowly making progress until I joined back up with the streets in Hollywood.

An early goal had been to get a good photo of the Hollywood sign up on the hill. I saw it often, always far away, and then actually turned off my route toward it through some very heavy traffic. I noticed the tour buses climbing a big hill and realized that I was on Sunset Boulevard, near a section called Sunset Strip, reminiscent of "77 Sunset Strip." The traffic was so thick that it was barely moving, and UPS drivers were walking the packages long distances for delivery. I finally got on the sidewalk myself and got out of there with only a few distant pictures of the Hollywood sign. A couple of interesting facts about the sign included that the letters are 50 feet tall and that the caretaker for the whole sign used to live in one of the letters. Universal Studios was close by, and so was the Hollywood Walk of Fame.

Next, after a winding and sometimes hilly ride on Sunset Boulevard, were several signs pointing toward Dodger Stadium. I knew which direction the stadium was, but did not take time to go find it. An American League stadium would have enticed me to do it for sure. Regardless, the climbing had begun. After leaving the beach area, I had to climb quickly up and over the Santa Monica Mountains.

A driver chose to blow his horn at me for not moving quickly enough at a stop light in Pasadena. The event marked my first horn in anger or something close to it for this trip. For sure, it would not be the last. I was studying my map a little ahead of the next turns during one of the eternal stoplights that I had encountered all morning, and a driver with Texas plates was bothered by my minor delay.

Pasadena was still quite pretty and the site for the Tournament of Roses Parade each New Year's Day. But more importantly, it was also the site of the first cheeseburger. A grill chef called his invention "the first cheese hamburger" in 1924.

I also saw the Santa Anita horse racing track in Arcadia where Seabiscuit made his amazing comeback. The race track was also used as an internment and detention camp for Japanese Americans during World War II. The Marx Brothers made a movie here called "A Day at the Races."

One of my goals as I read more about Route 66 and some of its history, especially the early history, was to spend as many nights as possible in the older motels. The first opportunity came as I pedaled past Arcadia into Glendora. After so many stoplights for the day, and it seeming that I was off the bike more than I was on it, I decided to stop after 53 miles at the 20th Century Motor Lodge. Although built in 1947, I thought of the motel as old, but it still looked great.

After a nice talk with Manager Sherrie Berillion during which I got pointers on other, much older motels to visit, I noticed pictures on the wall of Ronald Reagan, Doris Day and Richard Nixon. It was also the first time I heard of motels being referred to as cottage style, meaning the motel was divided into multiple individual buildings, usually with one or two rooms each. The motel was perfect for a cyclist, although it was just the first of the motels with WiFi that would work in one place and not another.

Sherrie sent me to a Route 66-style diner called Legends that was too expensive and certainly hawking food that would not power my bike ride too far. Still, to get in the spirit of things, I ordered a small amount and soaked up the atmosphere of the place.

Many more challenging miles lay ahead, complete with extreme temperatures soon. At Glendora, my elevation was about 900 feet - just a drop in the bucket to where we will climb soon. I had already ridden through cities in this first day with populations of close to four million people. My two-lane adventure had started, and I already thought that this ride had the potential to be something special. Bobby Troup had written "Get Your Kicks on Route 66" back in the 1940s, and although his song visualized driving westward into the sunset, I was going eastward toward the sunrise and with the wind behind me more than not. This truly was going to be a great adventure!

CHAPTER (3)

Heading toward the heat and the hills

was almost anxious to get started on both the heat and the hills. They were both just ahead and it was time to tackle them, facing head-on the hardest parts of this adventure, before too much longer.

I enjoyed my first real night on the road, although the riding was not very challenging yet and the distance for the day was more like warm-up mileage. Still, in varying degrees, I was getting re-immersed into one of my favorite activities. The bike seemed perfect, although my legs may have grown longer because an adjustment had to be made to raise the seat higher on the bike. Or they didn't grow longer, and the seat was just installed too low in Santa Monica. That was most likely the real answer.

Out of the motel in Glendora, I noticed right away that the road had started to climb more as I continued east. San Dimas, a beautiful little town, was next up, and my maps called for riding the Pacific Electric Trail. Here was where I could get into trouble with Adventure Cycling. Trail riding, especially the greenway type, usually limited any views of the passing towns and of Route 66 itself. After trying it for about an hour, I stopped and talked with Mike Beadwood of Rancho Cucamonga, a retired railroad worker from the area. I told Mike that I wanted to ride the roads and streets and asked how to get back on Route 66. I also asked if there was any reason not to get back on the streets, specifically whether there was something that I would miss if not on the greenway. Mike assured me that I would be fine back on Route 66, and he told me how to do it, plus he expressed concern that the forecast dangerous heat wave was coming. I told Mike that I had already taken precautions to be prepared for the heat. Mike said, "California and Arizona are supposed to be really in for it, and you are headed for the worst of it."

Back on the Rancho Cucamonga streets, I was happy to find great bike lanes and plenty of good and courteous drivers. So far, California drivers had been about as nice as I have seen anywhere. The city was once a huge ranch and was named for a Shoshone word for "Sandy Place." I headed for Fontana, another big California city, and then on to San Bernardino.

Local merchants were piling on the Route 66 theme, and for the first time, I began to see some serious restorations. One station, the Cucamonga Service Station, still had the sign that was displayed when it was shut down offering gasoline for 17 cents per gallon. Even Denny's and McDonald's were decorated in Route 66 themes, and a large number of older motels from the era lined the streets. The first McDonald's was here in 1948. I did notice almost as soon as I left town that the pace and amount of traffic relaxed quite a bit. For the first time, I had left behind the city traffic.

I followed Route 66 out of San Bernardino, and then the climbing began. I was soon to climb over those mountains that I had seen ahead for the last two days. A steady climb of about eight miles and then a serious one for a mile before settling back to steady again for eight miles was making me work, especially at the beginning of one of these long adventures. It usually takes about ten days to get my muscles used to the hard climbing. Also for the first time, but certainly beginning a regular habit, I had to ride on the interstate to continue the path of the original Route 66. The State of California signs directed me onto the breakdown lanes of I-15. At the same time, the serious climbing began in earnest. Eight more miles upward continued on interstate riding, all in the lowest possible gear. One exciting highlight came when a tractor-trailer had blocked the whole breakdown lane on a heavy traffic day. I had to jump off the bike, dash around the truck and hop quickly back into the breakdown lane to continue on. As always in these situations, the crest of the climbing finally came, this time at the Cajon Summit as the elevation reached 4,190 feet. Just a day and a half ago, I was at sea level on Santa Monica Beach. Also in this area was the intersection of Route 66 and the Pacific Coast Trail, a hiking trail along much of the highest altitudes between the Mexican and Canadian borders.

Next, I was forced to get back off the interstate in an area where a service road exists, and I found another pattern that would persist off and on until reaching Chicago. Mariposa was the service road with paving as bad as I had encountered in any of my previous rides, so rough that at times it was actually hard to stay on the bike. I did almost lose control of it once, not surprising since signs and maps said "Rough Road," and the maps said to make sure everything was securely bolted down. Never have I ridden on such a road, and I hope not to again.

For my second night on the road, I spent the evening at the New Corral Motel in Victorville. Victorville was a nice town, very modern and paved well, just past the horrendous stretch of road previously mentioned. The New Corral Motel, built in the 1940s, had a big neon sign with a symbol of Trigger, Roy Rogers' famous Palomino, on the top of it. Rogers used to have a museum nearby before it was moved to Branson, Missouri. Without much prodding, I had already decided that this historic motel thing would be fun, but I was expecting to get bitten eventually with a bad experience of some sort. The New Corral was great and close to a nice grocery store, just my kind of place.

Rogers, the "King of the Cowboys" and Dale Evans, "Queen of the West" spent their retirement years near here. Since passing through Victorville, I have looked at the terrain on the old Roy Rogers shows, and it certainly resembled the scenery in that area.

The land had changed, as well as the terrain. There were no naturally occurring trees, and much of the minimal growth was just scrub brush. Just as the temperature started to get hotter, the real shade had left the area. There was no unirrigated grass, either. I was now in the desert.

In retrospect, one of the funniest things that happened on the complete Route 66 ride occurred on this Victorville day. I knew that the grocery store was around but could not see it, so I walked over to a young couple who seemed to be about to get in their car. Admittedly now looking a little dirty and scruffy, I started to ask about the store, but before I said a thing, the man replied, "No we don't have any spare change!" I quickly told him, "No, I just wanted to ask where the grocery store is. I am staying at the motel and the desk clerk told me the grocery was close by." It was worth a good laugh afterwards.

With that, I bought some ice cream and began to think about how to prepare for the heat. It was just a couple of days away. I planned a very early start for the next few days, hoping to get on the road as soon as I could see and be seen. My new flashing red light was not doing well and for some reason would not keep running and a change of batteries had not helped. I only needed it to be flashing for an hour or two each morning, but at this point I thought it was only working for a half hour or so, and maybe less.

Still, the light came on and looked fine as I headed out toward Oro Grande with a very small and unawake business district. Someone had done a great job of setting up a forest of bottle trees.

Bottle trees are any kind of wooden or metal stands, similar to coat racks, that can hold a bunch of empty bottles turned upside down.

On to Hellendale, the home of the Exotic World Burlesque Hall of Fame. Admission was free, perfect for me, but I was way too early to get in. On to Barstow, a town of just over 20,000 but with at least 20 motels. Nearly all of the motels, and lots of other businesses, touted Route 66, a process becoming more common as I rode farther east. Also in Hellendale was a very elaborate McDonald's with a huge water tower and a place where the patrons could eat inside old rail cars. While in town, I stopped at a Dollar General to get some more batteries with the hope they might help my flashing red light to be more consistent and another battery for my cyclometer should I need it.

More little towns followed as I pedaled into Daggett, only notable for an 1880s hotel where Tom Mix once stayed. On to Newberry Springs, where two convenience stores dominated the town. I learned later that Newberry Springs was once called "Water Town" because it supplied the only water to the next crossroads called Ludlow.

Since I decided to spend the night in Ludlow at a truck stop motel, a few locals supplied me some more interesting information about the area. Until 1988, the residents did not have dial phones. They simply picked up the phone, and an operator from faraway Los Angeles or San Bernardino came on the line to help them. On an incoming call, every resident had a distinct ring, and only that resident was supposed to answer.

My overnight in Ludlow followed a toasty 92 miles as the major heat wave had begun to arrive. Part of my ride that day was again on the interstate because the current Route 66 road surface was so bad. A very rough nine-mile section caused me to rejoin the interstate with more super-slab riding to come over the next few days. Of course, the road surface on I-40 is good. The traffic was moderate and, at least in this case, I was glad to ride the interstate. "Share the Road" signs were scattered along the road, and my map said that interstate riding is legal due to an earlier agreement allowing cyclists to connect the scattered existing portions of Route 66.

The train tracks were now close to the roads that I was riding, and it was a pleasant thing for me to see so many trains coming by. The railway often took the very best terrain for its tracks, and the interstate got the next best. Route 66, where the existing road remained, did not minimize the terrain at all. It looked to me like the pavement had been put down over the terrain exactly as it existed, probably the quickest way to do it. I imagine that a large part of Route 66 travelers in the heyday years had plenty of trains visible beside America's Highway.

My love affair with Dairy Queen on Route 66 started in Ludlow. Just as I neared Ludlow, I saw the DQ sign on one end of the little town as I looked for the truck stop and the motel where I planned to stay. A short uphill ride took me to the main area of Ludlow around the truck stop where I checked into the motel. A restaurant caught my attention, and I asked how long it stayed open. The convenience store clerk said, "Oh, it depends on business. They should still be open." Apparently, there was no set time, so I stopped in to check the menu. Paying too much for a grilled cheese and some fries was only going to be the prerequisite for my first pineapple milkshake at DQ. I had to attack the serious heat the next day and looked forward to some ice cream. Needles, one of the hottest places on earth, was on tap for tomorrow.

After I ate and submitted my daily report back to the paper, I went outside to walk around. Although Ludlow was hot, it was still significantly cooler than what I would experience over the next two days. The sunset, as it dropped below the mountains that I had just climbed, was going to be worth seeing. Plus, I needed to spend some time walking in my good sandals. My toes tended to hurt some late in the day, especially when hard climbing was involved. Walking in the sandals seemed to help quite a bit. The walking also helped with my restlessness about the extreme heat coming. There was some mining equipment next to the restaurant, and I walked over to take a few photos of it. A plaque mentioned that leftover nuclear bombs from the Cold War era were considered for demolition of the rock formations in the area during interstate construction. Thankfully, they were not used.

Earlier in this chapter, I mentioned that I stopped in Barstow at a Dollar General to get some batteries. While there, two ladies were in front of me buying a few things and some ice. I thought nothing of it at the time, but as I walked around this evening, I spotted those two ladies again as they were taking pictures of the same mining equipment near the restaurant. After telling them where I first saw them, Tere Tangeman and Barbara Polson, from San Diego, told me that they too were riding part of Route 66. We had a nice talk and made pictures in the near dark before they rode off to find a motel near Needles.

Before going to bed shortly thereafter, I decided that I would jump on I-40 and head east at 4:30 a.m. My map for the area called for the strong possibility of there being at least one bridge out on Route 66, and with the looming heat, I did not want to backtrack. If the bridge was out, I would spend at least 30 miles trekking back to the interstate, so I just planned to put more of the odds in my favor. There was no real scenery to see along Route 66 in this area anyway.

Up at 3:30 a.m. and heading for the interstate on-ramp after stocking up at the truck stop, I was surprised to see a sign that prohibited bicycles. This time, the only real option for me was to stick with my original plan and claim ignorance once stopped, if in fact that sign was correct. I rode confidently onto the interstate and re-alized that the breakdown lane was very dark. There was no choice but to pedal ahead and look hard for any obstructions since I hoped to see them in time to stop or move over. Those usual large chunks of tires were definitely out there and were certainly big enough to pitch me off the bike. I did narrowly miss something that looked like a rubber roll.

Just after the roll, I saw another "Share the Road" sign and knew it was OK to be on this section of the interstate. My biggest dilem-ma was that the road between Ludlow and Needles had virtually no supply points, especially with the bridge likely out. I missed Siberia — an unusual name for such a hot area — and Amboy because of the bridge. There was a small store in Amboy kept open by a kind person who was doing a service for the area.

The scenery as I pedaled along was very much all desert. I did pass an exit for Essex Road, near the area where General Patton trained his tank troops before going to battle with famed German General Erwin Rommel in Africa during World War II. Next was a well-placed rest area that I visited but found the water warm and tepid, not as good as the water in my bags. A small convenience store was at the next exit, but I had a lot of water loaded in the bags of the bike and it was early enough in the day that I just kept riding.

Major Rocky Mountain-style climbing was the constant for much of the next 16 miles as I reached the top of the pass that sent me barreling downhill toward Needles. Once across the pass, I sensed the air temperature warming quickly as I descended toward town. Off in the distance, I could see a green ribbon that included the town. Also, as I started to pick up the pace toward Needles, the headwind became so fierce that I still had to pedal at times to keep moving forward.

Home of Charles Schultz of "Peanuts" fame, Needles is known

for being hot. However, the closer I got, the more lush and green it looked with the Colorado River running through the town. I had often wondered what would bring people to this place in the middle of the desert, and the river filled the bill.

All cyclists were instructed to exit from I-40 onto existing pavement from Route 66, pavement that looked like it had been neglected for 40 years. After about a little more than a mile, I entered better pavement at the town limits. At this point, I didn't know how hot the actual temperature was but I knew that I was HOT! I saw a Dairy Queen and decided to get a milkshake and sit down in the shade and figure out my next move. In line in front of me was a grandmother, a mom and daughter. All of them were struggling to decide what to order, especially the little girl. Finally, they placed their order and it was so complicated and long that I got my milkshake while they were standing around waiting.

Finally refreshed after slowly downing the milkshake, I rode on into town and found a Budget Inn that seemed nice and had a good price. I checked in and found the air conditioner already running and realized that I had lived through 93 miles on the hottest day that I had ever experienced. The motel owner said that 117 degrees was predicted, but I don't think it got higher than 114! After hugging the AC for the next hour while I submitted my report for the day, I felt much better and decided to walk back to the DQ and get another milkshake and some other food for the evening. By this time, the wind had died down and it was just bright and hot. Still, the walk was fine, and I returned with plenty to eat while I planned for an even hotter day coming up tomorrow. Another early start and the roll-up water bottles both helped make that day doable.

Needles got its name from some rocky outcroppings just across the Colorado River in Arizona. The river bath scene for "Grapes of Wrath" was filmed here. Marking the eastern edge of town was an

DAVID FREEZE

old and very stout wagon that was likely used as the 20-mule team wagon in "Death Valley Days," which starred Ronald Reagan. I remember waking up during the night a couple of times and stepping outside, quickly realizing that the overnight temperatures were still hot in the low 90s.

As I was about to leave California, I thought of what the first sight of the state might have been like for those who were betting their futures and dreams on the land to the west that I had just crossed. Those travelers had just crossed serious desert and there was still plenty more ahead. The actual crossing point for Route 66 over the Colorado took several routes during the road's heyday, but I had to jump back on I-40 to make my crossing. Back on the bike early, but not quite as early as the day before, I pedaled out of town east into more of the Mojave Desert.

I had plenty of water in my bags and I only intended to ride about 70 miles, much less than the day before. The maps gave us two options: one that would follow Interstate 40 and another that would go cross-country on some portions of the actual Route 66. I rode right out of Needles and began to follow a hilly road away from the interstate and realized that it would just take me back across more barren terrain later. I turned around and headed back to I-40 to cross into Arizona, where I could get a good view of the river and a picture of the state sign.

The Colorado River was still amazing to me. I had seen so little that was green for several days now, and the river made the area around it look so inviting. Crops and trees made me imagine something similar to North Carolina. Approaching the river, I saw the Arizona sign and planned to continue on the interstate and be in Kingman by early in the afternoon. Over the river was a spectacular white suspension bridge, built in 1916, that was only used to support a pipeline and no roads.

As soon as I crossed into Arizona, my plans changed. The breakdown lane was the worst paving that I had been on yet and was simply unrideable, remaining that way for as far as I could see. I had no choice but to ride off the exit ramp toward Oatman. I rode briefly beside the river on a flat plain but knew any flat area would not last long. A small fox came out of the brush, looked at me and then went back into the brush. After he stuck his head out again, I stopped to take a photo of him just about the time a car came too fast around the curve. I jumped back and dropped my iPad on the pavement, barely able to keep my balance on the bike. Of course, the fox ran and was not seen again. Luckily, the iPad still worked and didn't seem damaged. I got myself squared away and almost immediately started on an uphill grade. It was a sign of things to come.

The Colorado River in the Needles, California, area was at about 400 feet in elevation, and what I dreaded on the alternative route was the incredible climbing in the quickly building heat. I rode on and stopped at a small convenience store in Golden Shores, where I was warned about taking on the climbing ahead during such heat. The clerk said, "Nobody ever rides a bicycle to Oatman except in the early morning or late afternoon." I thanked her but had no choice except to continue but as I rode by the fire department, I wondered if I might be seeing those guys later.

Back in the full-fledged desert, I rode along, steadily climbing at a steeper rate as it got hotter. Very little was interesting about the terrain, and there was even a notation on my maps that a row of electrical towers was halfway. By the time I finally made those towers, I had used up nearly all of my water. More, in fact, than what I used during the entire full day before. It was over 100 degrees at 10 a.m., and there was no breeze.

I continued to pedal, and a van driver stopped to ask me if I was

OK and offered water. That was one of the best-tasting bottles of water that I had ever taken, but I assured her that I was fine. Nearly all of the riding was in the lowest gears by this time, and I admittedly was struggling and thought that maybe I should have said so. In four hours, I had climbed from 400 feet to about 3,000 feet, all of it on a rough road.

Finally, just after noon, I made it to Oatman, Arizona. When I had first considered the shorter, easier, and therefore quicker route on the interstate, I was sorry that I would miss Oatman. Now, I only wanted desperately to get to the little town named after a white girl named Olive Oatman who was kidnapped by Indians, probably the Tolkepayas. She was sold to the Mojave Indians and forced to live with them for several years. Oatman was a rich mining town until World War II and now sustained itself with tourism.

As I rode into Oatman, I saw hundreds of people walking around in an Old West town. I had read that the town is not only historic but has rekindled itself into the town that it was in the late 1800s. Besides people, I saw a dozen or so wild burros, although they looked about as tame as could be. A brief stop at a gift store for bottled water gave me a chance to cool off a little and process all of this. It was now early afternoon, well over 100 degrees, and I still had more than 30 miles to make it to Kingman. Added to all this, the gift shop owner told me that I would encounter steep switchbacks heading out of town, and the next ten miles would be harder than the climb from Needles. Forecasts called for the highest temperatures of the heat wave over the following two to three days.

My daughter had asked me to make good decisions on this trip, particularly where the heat was concerned. I knew that my body did not need another four to five hours of tough conditions on this day. A quick inquiry to the gift store owner opened the door to renting a cabin above the town. I was directed to the hotel and specifically the bar where several cabins were listed for rent. On the way, I was able to watch a good gunfight on Main Street. Then I took the cheapest cabin and had to push the bike up a dusty and rutty road to it. A long way up to it! Right away, I found that the AC unit could not cool the place in the extreme heat, and I was transferred to another, bigger cabin. This one was at the top of the hill but with a better central air unit that eventually began to cool the place. Local water was not drinkable, and bottled water was provided. I was finally settled in Arizona after just 42 of the toughest miles I have ever cycled. But it was the right decision. I headed out to find out more about this town of 125 residents. The rest of Arizona was just ahead.

CHAPTER 4

Getting to the heart of this adventure

Now that the hills and the heat were a part of my Route 66 adventure, the long ride began in earnest. With a mid-afternoon temperature hovering close to 110 in Oatman, Arizona, I went out to explore the town while my new cabin's air conditioner began its work to cool the interior.

Those burros wandered around everywhere, looking for anything to eat, especially the burro food sold in dispensers along Main Street. I stopped at the general store to get a gallon of water and some snacks and went back to the bar at the Oatman Hotel to see what was on the menu. The bar was the only place in town for sandwiches, and they made a veggie burger. While there, I looked in on the honeymoon suite of Carole Lombard and Clark Gable from 1939. Oatman has a big day scheduled each year when the town hosts its annual Egg Frying Contest. Any solar powered gizmo is acceptable, and the number of tourists sometimes increases tenfold for the event. Parts of "How the West Was Won" from the 1960s were filmed in Oatman.

Late in the evening, just before dark, I noticed what I thought was a dog looking in the front door of my newer cabin. A closer look showed that the dog was actually a coyote ambling slowly around the mountaintop. I was bothered because I thought that I had lost one of my good sandals and would either be without or have to buy another pair later. Those sandals were the perfect pair for me, comfortable and supportive too, plus they were now along for their third ride.

After a restful night inside, I left the cabin to go back down the steep hill at 4:45 a.m. to begin the day's climb out of town. The gift shop owner had earlier mentioned and the cycling map confirmed the climb to be extreme, but first I wanted to get down the steep hill with the bike still standing up. The road was all dirt with several turn-offs, and I just walked the bike along in the dark, holding the brakes to keep it from slipping. I saw a dark spot and picked up the missing sandal, brushed it off and put it back in one of my panniers. Back on Main Street, I saw the burros still walking around while looking for yet another handout. A couple of them turned toward me, and I just rode away, leaving them to wait for the day's tourists.

The low temperature was in the upper 80s, and I knew that the upcoming morning would be another tough one. The climb ahead of me was going to be even tougher than yesterday, but at least the sun would not get over the mountains for a while. The series of switchbacks that the gift shop owner told me about were so steep in places that all I could do was push the bike. I had close to 25 pounds of water on the bike and no choice but to bring that much along since I had nearly ran out the day before. Back and forth, back and forth, I pushed toward the sunny spot at the top of Sitgreaves Pass. Near the top, where I could look back and see the long, winding road below me, I heard some rustling in the brush and saw two more wild burros. For some reason, I thought that the manure along the sides of the road came from horses but realized the wild burros wandered the road at the higher elevations, too. These two burros didn't approach like their cousins in town, and I took a few minutes to drink plenty of water and eat a snack after topping the pass. I just had beaten the sun to the spot.

During Route 66's heyday, towing companies were kept busy

pulling cars over the top of this pass. I read that many of the cars and trucks made the climb in reverse because reverse was geared lower than first forward in the standard manual transmission. I remembered only one climb over a pass in the Rockies that was this steep and challenging.

Near the top of the pass was the modern, working Colorado Mine that had once been closed except for tours. The price of gold went back up, and the mine was reopened, improved and was hard at work as I passed by. In fact, the only traffic of the morning had been workers in their pickup trucks headed for the mine. Several blocked-off older mines were also visible.

My next goal was the town of Kingman, where I had originally planned to spend the previous night. The ride down on the other side of the pass was much easier, with lots of coasting and only a few segments of short climbing. I saw a few shelters and abandoned homes and businesses. The terrain was a little greener than around Oatman, although most of the green was from a few mosses and small scrub plants.

About ten miles from anywhere in either direction, I found a beautifully renovated old service station offering snacks, groceries and cabins along the nearly deserted road. It had yet to open for the morning, so I missed a chance to see inside. I could not help but think how likely I would have been in one of those cabins last night had I persisted in forging ahead in Sunday's 110-degree desert heat. The result could have been much worse had I decided to continue riding on Sunday afternoon. I was certainly convinced that the decision not tackle Sitgreaves Pass until this morning was the right one.

I rode easily into Kingman as the temperature climbed to about that same level again. I had heard about the fantastic Route 66 Museum in the restored Kingman Powerhouse building and planned all along to see it. There was no place to put the bike in the shade, but I did take an hour to view the museum. Plenty of old vehicles, some of them used in mock-ups of how the passengers headed west in search of a better life, highlighted the museum. Dusty and dirty parents and kids, all riding in a Jed Clampett type truck with all their hopes and dreams for a better life ahead. Newsreels and newspapers gave insight into the hardships of traveling America's Highway west. I recommend this museum as one of the best since it did not focus solely on one area or state. By my count, there were at least 20 Route 66 museums along the entire route.

After leaving the Powerhouse, I realized that my ticket also was good for entry into the Mojave Museum. This museum did highlight the wide and varied history of the Kingman area. A huge display on the Indians of the area and another on the harsh life of the working cowboy were both amazing.

I was surprised to read that there may be as many as 100,000 abandoned mines in the area. Ten years prior to my visit, two girls fell down an abandoned shaft, and one of them was killed. Not just gold was mined, with lead, copper, silver and other metals native to the area.

Also in the museum was a big display on Roy Rogers. Of course, I grew up when Rogers and Dale Evans had their popular TV show. While in the first mountain cabin in Oatman, I watched two of their half-hour shows and found them as good as ever. Since Rogers spent so much time in the area, that may be the reason for what appeared to be a local Roy Rogers TV channel.

One of Rogers' sidekicks on TV and in ten of his movies was Andy Devine. Devine was the favorite native son of Kingman and was honored with Andy Devine Avenue, the town's main drag. Devine acted in over 400 films.

Finally, I noticed an exhibit in the museum about the 7,000 post-

World War II planes that were brought to Kingman Army Airfield for dispersal. Most were heavy, long-range bombers. A few of the planes were sold to Americans but most were sold for scrap to an investor. Rumors later persisted that the investor got his money back just from reclaiming the fuel from the planes.

I looked around a little more at the most interesting town of the trip so far, then decided to call it a day after just 33 miles, my shortest day of the entire Route 66 adventure. My motel was another old one called the Hill Top Motel. When I checked in about 2 p.m., the air temperature was 117, which I am pretty sure was the hottest official temperature that I endured along the historic highway. The air conditioner worked well, and I got my food and other supplies from the Walgreens next door. While the outside temperature cooled to 112 by late that afternoon, I still hoped that the climbing slated for the next several days would take me to cooler temperatures. Kingman was a great place to capture the western culture and history of Route 66 and to gather information on what to expect when I left town. Although only a small part of the TV series "Route 66" was actually filmed on the famous highway, two rooms at the Kingman Quality Inn were named for George Maharis and Martin Milner, the show's stars. Others who passed this way for guest appearances were Alan Alda, Robert Duvall, Joey Heatherton and Burt Reynolds. Clark Gable and Carole Lombard got married in the local Methodist church before hustling over to Oatman for their honeymoon. I would have hustled the other way based on the present-day conditions.

With a little longer afternoon than normal in Kingman, I had a chance to research my route for the next couple of days. Reasonably priced motels seemed to be few and far between, but by now I had confidence that I could figure something out if need be. My tent and sleeping bag were ready to be used, although I could hardly imagine using them on an early evening that would still be easily over 100 degrees.

The next morning, I headed east out of Kingman before daylight with the nighttime low of 85 degrees still in place. My plan was to stay on Route 66 all day, no turns to leave it or detours onto the interstate. My prayers included the hopes of some clouds, a few drops of rain and a tailwind.

My first stop for the day was at a modern, but not busy, convenience store in Valle Vista. A local contractor came over to talk as I got off the bike and leaned it against the wall. By the way, my Surly does not have a kickstand so that is why all the pictures show it leaning against something. Long-distance bikes don't usually come with a kickstand, but I am not sure exactly why although I suspect that it has something to do with proper balancing of the heavy load. The contractor warned me about the intense heat and told me to take a day off somewhere just like his workers were doing. I thanked him but said that I planned to keep going and would take precautions. By this time, I had already experienced hotter temperatures than what was forecast for this day.

I rode on and found the road a continuous up and down, some of the climbs steep but not long. On one of the curvy uphills, I found the Hackberry General Store, probably the most unusual store of any kind up to this point. The store has a collection of Route 66 memorabilia, most of it probably for sale. There was a red Corvette and plenty of other vintage cars. I saw a urinal mounted on the outside of the building and a sign that said, "All hippies must enter by the back door. No kidding!" I enjoyed looking around but decided against staying another hour until the store opened. One person told me that the store had been in and out of business since Route 66 first came through the area.

I rode on through Valentine, where Peter Fonda fixed a flat in

"Easy Rider," but nothing was moving today, and into Truxton, the site of a fantastic convenience store with plenty of Route 66 memorabilia and farm supplies. With the heat already building, I bought plenty of water and some snacks, including a giant cinnamon roll and an energy-giving ice cream sandwich, then went out to sit in the shade for a few minutes before pedaling on. The bathrooms were outside and so was plenty of old farm machinery and historic vehicles. This was the first place that I had seen square hay bales with three strings. Since it hardly rains in this area, farmers and ranchers don't have much hay but what they do have is very expensive. Often, the high-priced hay is stacked outside near where it will be fed to the horses or cows.

My farm has produced hay for years, and it is always interesting to me to see how hay is grown and baled in other areas. When I first imagined the bicycling trip through the desert, I had no idea that there would be any hay production. Irrigation costs must have been justified to grow the high-priced, but good-quality hay.

I went back inside to ask about why the motel just down the road had closed. It was listed as still open in my guidebook and maps, so I thought there might be a story. The clerk told me that a new group came in and began a big-time renovation, then when it seemed like they were doing well, they pulled the plug and shut things down. I found not one, but two closed-up motels across from each other. Traffic was still very light, and I imagined that it just about always was.

By this time, I began to think more earnestly about where I might spend the night. I passed through Peach Springs on the Hualapai Indian Reservation where I was offered a room for the night for $200. Of course, I declined but still wondered what made the room so special. The fun continued as I stopped by the Grand Canyon Caverns where I had called the night before and been offered another overpriced room. I stopped by long enough to verify the price and look at the motel. While I got a bottle of water without a sticker on it and was charged $2.85, a discussion was being held about where putt-putt players could actually drink and why they had to stay away from certain areas if inebriated. I still felt good, and Seligman was only another 25 miles farther east, plus I knew it was a Route 66 town. On I pedaled.

I passed a couple of places where the Grand Canyon could be seen briefly far in the distance. Also about this time, I saw a little black pouch on the side of the road that appeared to hold a cyclist jacket. I rode back and picked it up, wondering who might have lost it. I never opened the pouch but slipped it into my bag.

The afternoon had gradually become a little cloudy, and more good things were happening, too. Although I was still climbing, the tail wind that I had hoped for had arrived and was doing good work. The climbing was not harsh, and the day was turning out much easier than I earlier thought it might. Storm clouds, the first of my journey, had started building to the northeast. As I neared Seligman, I felt better and better.

Two unusual things occurred during the afternoon. I saw two cyclists lying under what looked like thin tarps beside Route 66. This was mid-afternoon, very bright and hot, and about the last time that a nap would seem proper. It was so interesting that I stopped and snacked while watching them for a short while. Each person, genders unknown, was separately under the tarp cover and seemed to roll occasionally. Maybe they planned to ride at night, but I will never know. Their antics were not worth staying around for.

The other thing was that on all my previous rides, there have been lots of traveling motorcyclists. Seldom do they pay any attention to a lone cyclist. On this trip, in these conditions, I seemed to get a wave from most of the ones that passed by. Possibly, they just thought, "This guy might be a little crazy!" Either way, it was fun to wave back as I rode by at 10-12 mph.

A highlight for the day was a chance meeting with Deborah McIntosh and Teresa Albertus, both from Colorado Springs, Colorado. They had been riding Route 66 west from Albuquerque in their car and hoped to dip their toes in the Pacific near Santa Monica soon. We had all stopped to take the same picture of an old service station and enjoyed a nice conversation that included their visit by train to the Grand Canyon. Both ladies encouraged me to take the time to do the same.

Next a little windblown rain fell, just enough to see and feel it. The wind swirled, and at times, just as I crested the latest hill at 5,250 feet, it pushed me sideways and backwards. Then as the storms passed by, the wind settled back into a tailwind as I rode into Seligman. Seligman is Route 66, through and through. From one end to the other, stores, shops, restaurants and motels flaunt the road's name. A local businessman, Angel Delgadillo, was responsible for the recent rebirth of the famous road by using his contacts to facilitate the coordination between other towns, states, federal officials and agencies to ease the travel of vehicles and yes, bikes, as they cruised his road.

With my motel search looking better but still not settled, I stopped at the first one right next to the Road Kill Café and asked about a room. The price was much higher than I expected, so I checked at a few more places and took the cheapest. My choice was a poor one but not dreadfully so as eventually the small AC unit mustered up the ability to cool the room later in the evening. I actually had to change rooms because the first one never gained any cooling advantage. All at the end of 87 miles for the day.

The owner of the motel had trouble with his WiFi, but he made up for it by sending me with a discount to a local restaurant with breakfast all day and vegetarian choices. The waitress told me right away that only a few breakfast items were still available, which I didn't understand, and ordered the veggie burger. It was a good choice and included an enjoyable conversation with the waitress who probably wondered why I didn't shave. For some reason, I had been on the road a week and had not yet shaved.

Back at the room with my food and some snacks from the newly opened Family Dollar, I had a good night. I won't name the motel, but once the night came, things were fine.

Out again so very early that nothing was moving and my still-faulty red flashing light could be seen, I had a shorter day planned because about 50 miles of riding should take me to Williams, the stepping off point for the Grand Canyon. Williams was also the home of the Grand Canyon Railway and near the top of some very serious climbing.

I also left Seligman with an opinion on their motels. They are plentiful, but pricey. And the proof on the morning that I left town was that there were very few cars in the parking lots of those motels. Convenience store items are also very costly, the highest that I had seen so far on this ride. California prices were cheaper and I did not understand why this small Arizona town had seemingly locked in higher prices. That issue might be fixed some with the new Family Dollar, because their prices seemed more moderate. Contrast that to the fact that Seligman seems to be the most Route 66-committed town yet, making me think that the approach for local merchants is to push the prices up to the tourists. Not sure that was a solid approach, but it was my concern no longer.

Leaving Seligman, I began to climb and climb seriously over some quiet country. This was serious, low gear, sweating and quads-hurting climbing. There was a stint of riding on Interstate 40 during which I was passed by a cyclist that I had seen a couple of days before. This cyclist had briefly spoken as he passed me the previous time and did again on this day. However, I could not understand his words. On we rode as he pulled away from me again, and I remembered the bike jacket that I found on the road. There was a good chance that the jacket belonged to this cyclist, but he was gone again.

I rode on to the exit off I-40 at Ash Fork where, amazingly, the cyclist was sitting on a bench with his shoes off at the only convenience store. I stopped beside him and introduced myself and met Bardo Weryor of Mainz, Germany. Bardo was visiting in the United States and riding from Los Angeles to Denver. He was unusual in that his bike was an ultra-lightweight, not the kind normally used for long-distance rides. I picked it up and couldn't believe how light it was. Bardo carried his gear in an overstuffed backpack that rode high on his back as he pedaled along, something that I would not have enjoyed at all. After we talked a little bit, I asked Bardo if he had lost a jacket and then watched his face light up. It was great fun to hand it back to him. Bardo said that the jacket was very expensive and it was the only one he had. Shortly afterwards, Bardo stopped by the bathroom and headed back out to the road. I never saw him again after we wished each other "Safe travels!"

Back to the interstate, I was climbing seriously again. So were the trucks beside me as they constantly downshifted to climb the long hills. I did notice that for the first time, cattle guards were installed on the interstate on-ramps. Since there were no interstate fences, all the cows had to do was walk around the cattle guards to access the interstate. Either way, I never noticed a cow near the interstate.

I made it to Williams after only 43 miles of riding, even less than I thought. Still, with the climbing, I was glad to get there and a little unsure of what I might find for motel possibilities. I had made several calls the previous night and was informed that this was high season in Williams and "No less-than-$100 motel rooms exist!" I found a great place at the Highlander, much less than $100 a night, and the best room to date. The owner was also fun to talk to and he made me think about staying an extra night after my return from the Grand Canyon. I told the owner that I was going to see what kind of deal I could strike to take the train to the canyon and whether it would be best to spend a second night.

Off to the train office, I found a very nice setting that included a big-time ticket office. There were all types of options, but I took the deal that Deborah and Teresa had told me about. Besides the train ticket, I got a bus ticket that would take me to several more viewing areas other than the train drop-off point. To a person, everybody concerned told me that the Grand Canyon was truly spectacular and I should not miss it. Now I was set to see the one major natural attraction along Route 66, similar to Niagara Falls the previous summer.

In 1901, the Atchison, Topeka and Santa Fe Railroad completed a branch line from Williams to the Grand Canyon Village, and the first sightseers jumped aboard that year. A one-way ticket was $3.95 for the 65-mile ride as opposed to a range of $65 to $215 for the round trip today. The train stopped operating in 1968 due to the popularity of the family car. It was renovated and began running again in 1989 and was now owned by the same company that operated the 297-room Grand Canyon Railway Hotel. The train trip remained virtually the same as it was 100 years ago. I looked forward to my own ride.

Now with about half an afternoon remaining to get to know Williams better, I walked all around the train station and found that this day's train would return about 5:30 p.m. I planned to be back to see it. The downtown area had a divided Route 66 with most of the shops and restaurants on the eastbound side. I took time to visit some of the souvenir stores and to watch a special cable ride that has two seats under a motorized cable car that is retracted to a distance of about 300 feet and then released to race back to the finish.

I met Glenn and Linda Morton from Maryville, Tennessee, right after we all bought tickets. Glenn worked in radio, and they both knew where Salisbury is. We talked about going to the Grand Canyon and the fact that we had heard that there would be a gunfight at 9 a.m. the following morning. Williams certainly has a lot going on and had become my favorite Route 66 town so far after having only seen it for a few hours. My decision was easy to spend the next day going to the canyon, stay an extra night in Williams and then hit the pedals hard the following morning as I continued east.

Another pleasant plus about my motel was that it sat right between another Dairy Queen and a full size Safeway grocery store and not far from a pancake house. I visited all of them and quickly was set for the next day. I did pass on one pancake for $5. A visit back to the train station to see the Grand Canyon Railway train return and more walking around the town, now complete with outdoor singers and neon lights, was a perfect ending to nice day that even had slightly cooler temperatures.

Even though I had set the alarm later, I was still startled awake the next morning at the usual 4:30 a.m. time thinking that I needed to be getting dressed for an early pedaling start. I dozed off again and woke the next time thinking my bicycle should be way on down the road. Still, I felt rested as I headed for the early morning gunfight prior to my train ride to the Grand Canyon. There would be no pedaling today.

Only one horse thief was killed by the Williams sheriff. He gave the bad guys a chance to fess up but they had no intention of coming clean. I think I looked back and even saw the "kilt" one get up and stumble off as we headed for the train and our assigned seats. The daily newspaper was in my seat as I got settled in near a large group of English citizens touring the U.S. We had a female conductor with a huge personality named Amber Rose and roving entertainers, all of them very good. The two-hour-plus train ride flew by, and I never once felt sleepy.

Arriving at the Grand Canyon, those of us that had extra tour tickets quickly boarded buses and had short stops at other scenic spots along the rim. One of them had a great view of the Colorado River a mile below. Some of the Grand Canyon stats included 1,904 square miles, ten miles wide, a mile deep and 2,757 miles in circumference. The park attracted more visitors and was photographed more than any other national park last year. I found the Grand Canyon simply amazing, nothing short of spectacular!

Right away, I saw pictures of the canyon at sunrise and sunset and knew that I would miss that opportunity on this visit. Also, the hike down into the very challenging Bright Angel Trail would be fun to do on another trip. A group of about 20 college freshmen made the return hike out of the canyon while I watched. It would have been so much fun to be there with them. Going down is easy, but just hiking back out without a backpack had them all very dirty and sweating profusely.

The Grand Canyon Village had a hotel, a historic lodge and plenty of other interesting things going on. One of the best on my day of visiting was a presentation of Indian hoop dances. I took my last 30 minutes and just gazed out at the spectacular mid-afternoon view from the rim area nearest the train. Ponderosa pines smelled like butterscotch and vanilla according to our conductor, and that smell was predominant in the loading area. I was familiar with a similar smell from previous Oregon and Maine cycling adventures.

Before the ride to the Grand Canyon, this part of Arizona looked much like Montana to me, very akin to the big sky country. Fifty miles to the horizon is probably a good estimate, and I do love scenery like that.

The ride back to Williams on the train was also very enjoyable. More entertainers stopped by and our "life of the party" conductor encouraged cowboy sing-alongs just before the previously shot-up bad guys from the morning shootout robbed the train. The Williams sheriff took care of the bad guys yet again.

Upon returning to Williams on the train, I missed a group of folks from home when they expected me to walk a different way to leave the train. Gary and Sylvia Ritchie from China Grove had followed my ride in the newspaper and happened to be in the area on family business and tried to find me. Later, the Ritchies had a train staffer leave me a message that I missed until they had already left town. Part of their trip out west included riding the posted parts of Route 66.

Another evening of just walking around the happening little town of Williams was fun, especially with yet another gunfight in the early evening street. Those streets seemed full of people, and everyone smiled as they strolled around town. I hoped to see Williams again on a return trip.

Already, I was thinking ahead. Trips to Winslow, the Painted Desert and the Petrified Forest were on my mind. Back to the room, back on the riding schedule, and it was time to get some sleep. Much more adventure was just around the corner.

My plan was to hit it hard, making a hard push east after a day off the bike. My first town was Flagstaff, and I liked what I saw even though it was early. My map was a little confusing, and I tried to follow the turns and proceeded to get lost. Without realizing it, I was headed back toward the Grand Canyon by a different route.

I knew that climbing was not supposed to be consistent this soon, and after about three miles, I stopped and asked a beer truck driver to help me. He said, "Oh man, you are way off track! It is miles from where you want to be." So, I followed his directions back the way that I had come and asked again. Same thing. A store operator told me that he had to think about how to get where I wanted to be. All that seemed pretty bad, but the fix was not hard at all. About six miles of total extra riding got me back on Route 66, and I still don't know exactly how I messed it up. Regardless, I saw plenty of Route 66 motels and restaurants. For the first time getting lost on this trip, the recovery was not bad.

While I knew very little of Flagstaff, I found out that the city came close to some movie notoriety when Cecil B. DeMille visited with hopes of starting his film industry here. On that very day, snow was falling, and DeMille changed his mind and headed to Hollywood.

I jumped back on I-40 east of Flagstaff for more desert riding. Route 66 had disappeared in much of the area and even the guidebook called for finding the interesting sites from the interstate. The first site was a giant crater about six miles off the interstate. A giant meteor was said to have crashed at about 45,000 mph to leave a crater that was 570 feet deep, a mile across and three miles in circumference. Just one day after seeing the Grand Canyon, another huge hole in the ground did not make an extra 12-mile ride seem worthwhile through the hot desert. At the time of this writing, I wish that I had taken the time to do it.

The second site was an abandoned group of buildings with two giant arrows pointed into the ground. Those arrows signified the name for the tourist complex known as Twin Arrows. Maybe more unusual was an attractive lady who was sitting beside the exit ramp in a chair and shaded by an umbrella. She had a notebook, some type of counter and a wonderful personality. I imagine that the pay might not have been worth the discomfort to count a minimal number of cars that passed by in the near-100-degree heat.

More excited than maybe I ought to be, I headed to Winslow, to the famous corner of Winslow, Arizona. The small town has latched onto the Eagles' classic song, "Take It Easy," for all its worth. Right away, I found "the corner," at the crossing of Kinsley and Second streets. A mural of "the girl," an actual flatbed Ford truck and a small park surrounding it all was my first stop in town. I read that the town has made an effort to revitalize the Route 66 area on both the one-ways of Second and Third streets.

A sidebar to the day was my visit to an exceptional Arizona rest area. With the extreme temperatures, brick-sided open shelters, as many as 20 of them at this rest area, were available for picnicking and just relaxing for weary or hungry travelers. Arizona does rest areas right.

After 102 miles for the day that included six miles of being lost, I planned to find my motel and spend the night planning the up-coming segment of my trip. Some more highlights were very near and so was New Mexico. I was having a wonderful time and had survived the worst of the heat. It was exciting to be on the road again!

CHAPTER 5

A rough end to Arizona and entering New Mexico

During an interesting evening at Earl's Motor Court in Winslow, Arizona, another of the Route 66-era motels with plenty of neon, I got some planning done. I spoke to the owner at length about the options for continuing east, and she told me that she had enjoyed the painted desert and the petrified forest in the past, but had not been to that area in several years. I had read that parts of the Petrified Forest National Park could be seen from Interstate 40 but really did not want to do it that way.

Earl's Motor Court was also one of the oldest motels along Route 66, and I understood that it had remained in the same family all along. My 1940s room was very basic with an ancient Hotpoint refrigerator that worked like a charm. The motel's postcard mentioned sleeping on the corner, but it was actually a couple of blocks away from the famous corner. Many of the businesses in downtown Winslow were closed, but clearly it had been a thriving town during Route 66's heyday. Proof of that was the La Posada Hotel, built in 1928 and restored in the 1990s to the grand style of yesterday and today with its guest rooms, gardens and meeting spaces.

A very early 5 a.m. departure heralded what I thought could be another challenging day. The early miles came on Interstate 40, and the option remained to continue with more of the same because only small segments of Route 66 remained in the area. After

I included the dilemma of how to spend this day in my evening prayers, the best answer was a commitment to the full effort to see the Petrified Forest National Park and the painted desert within it.

My first stop of the day was at the Jack Rabbit Trading Post, now just between the interstate and a segment of Route 66. The Jack Rabbit Trading Post once had signs all the way to Florida advertising how far it was to the Jack Rabbit. Those signs counted down the mileage to the trading post until the car finally arrived and everyone wanted to see what the fuss was about. A big jack rabbit out front with a saddle on it had been worn smooth by all the rabbit riders over the years. I hopped on the saddle too, of course, and became a rabbit rider myself.

The next town was Holbrook where I was able to join Route 66 again for the ride through town, the only relevant section around as far as I could tell. The well-known Wigwam Motel was on my right as I pedaled into town. Missing a night at the Wigwam was a major disappointment, even more so when I later found out how nice the inside of the teepees actually were. Originally, the first of seven Wigwam villages were built in 1933 and equipped with pay-per-listen radio. I was told that the Wigwam stayed full most nights and each of the teepees has a vintage vehicle parked next to it, too. Another "must do" for my next time through.

Near the middle of town, I spotted a bunch of huge and stoic dinosaur sculptures standing outside the Rainbow Rock Shop. The dinosaurs did not seem to move around much, but there was a sign on the lot that said, "Take personal photos at your own risk." The reason for the sign was not that the photographer was in any danger from the dinosaurs but from the owners who expected a fee for the photo opportunities. No one was around the place on this early Saturday morning, so I got my pictures for free without a hassle. The dinosaurs did not seem to mind at all.

A long and warm ride of 18 miles followed as I pedaled out to the Petrified Forest National Park. I had to buy a ticket from Park Ranger David Harmeil just before entering, the last time that I paid a full price ticket for a national park entry. A yearly park pass was definitely the right ticket for me as it proved useful throughout the rest of the ride. Early on, I had no idea that I would visit so many national parks during my Route 66 journey.

Before entering the park, I saw large amounts of petrified wood for sale beside the road. The owner of Earl's Motor Court told me that one piece of petrified wood was just like any other piece, so after entering the park on yet another hot day, I hoped to see more than just the wood. Interesting to me was that the petrified trees appeared to have been cut up and the large chunks were still on the ground in the shape of a tree. Had I thought of it, I would have asked later how they were cut just as a chain saw would have done. I did find out that the park was a dense and humid rain forest many eons ago, and some of the trees became mineralized versions of themselves.

The day had become quite hot by this time and the very challenging road was hard work. Traffic was light, and most people were driving slowly as I got deeper into the park. Large rock formations, often with varied colors and composition, became the order of the day.

Though quite amazing, the petrified wood and the rock formations were not all that I hoped to see. I had a brush with the Wind River Canyon in Wyoming during my 2013 ride, and I hoped that the painted desert might be nearly as good. The hills were tough and relentless, and I was starting to run low on water. I could hear the interstate sounds in the distance and knew that the end of the park was coming up. Soon, I saw a train pass through the park just before I rode over the interstate and thought, "Well, that was good, but not quite what I expected."

At that point, I thought that I would not have missed much had I just stayed with the interstate. At least my dehydrated self had that opinion at the time, but things soon changed. That last portion of the national park road, still challenging, began to offer viewing points of the fabulous painted desert. Several times, as far as I could see, the colorful rock and mineral deposit formations kept changing because of the sun and clouds marching across the area. It was spectacular — similar but still a little different from the Grand Canyon seen just a few days before. Immediately, I felt that the long ride through the hilly park had been worthwhile.

The very best viewing point was close to the exit of the park, and I waited longer there to watch more of the color show. I noticed that the park opened well after sunrise and closed before sunset, missing an opportunity to see those colors at possibly the peak times.

Then came an interesting dilemma for many who visit the park. Small pieces of the petrified wood were everywhere and easily picked up although it was illegal to do so. Just as I approached the exit to the park, there was a sign stating that all vehicles were subject to search before exit, and all of them were forced to stop to make sure they complied. I heard on the "Today" show several months ago that many people panicked and tossed out the pieces that they had picked up. I pulled up to the barricade and possible search of my bags and was waved immediately through. The park ranger probably knew that I had absolutely no interest in carrying even another half pound of weight.

Finally, at the end of the national park, I stopped in for some water and took time to make a call to the only motel in miles. So began one of the worst experiences of my journey and the only similar one in nearly 13,000 miles of long-distance cycling. I just did not know it yet. Before leaving the visitor center, I called the

Days Inn in Chambers. The evening before, I had called just to ask questions and to get a rate should I be able to reach Chambers this evening. This time, I told the girl my name and that I would make it to the motel if all went well and that I would see her in a couple hours. I also confirmed the rate, already one of the highest to date on this ride.

Back on the interstate and headed east again, I got a couple more views of the painted desert as the long and rolling hills continued. Route 66 had actually passed through a portion of the Petrified Forest National Park where a small pull-off and an abandoned gangster-type car marked the spot.

I kept riding, and at the end of 103 miles, I slowly pedaled into a small complex that had the Days Inn, an attached restaurant and a convenience store that sold fuel and gas, but no other businesses. This must have been Chambers, although I saw no confirmation of the fact. I stopped first at the high-priced convenience store and bought some Snapple and water. I was so thirsty and tired and had arrived later than I had hoped. Two women inquired about my ride and then another came over, too. The last one expressed concern that I had been out all day in the heat and wanted to know how she could follow my adventure. All of them were fun to talk to, but it was also time to get off my feet. The real fun was about to begin.

Confidently, I walked into the office and gave them my name. A guy, who later said he was the manager, first could not find my name, and once he did, his printer wouldn't work. He asked no questions and neither did the two other girls in the office. After a ten-minute delay, he finally handed me the room bill to sign, and I noticed that the rate was higher and also included no AAA discount. I told him about the agreed-upon rate and he replied that the rate was not good and that he had already included my discount even though it was not on the bill. I was trapped because it was very hot, the next motel was 30 miles away and the sun was already going down. Of course, this "manager" already knew this and actually told me, "Look, I am going to sell the room anyway. You can take or leave it!"

I thought about the situation while standing in front of the three of them, the two women still silent, and told him that this was a dishonest practice and that I would report him. He snickered and said, "Want the room or not?" I took the room, all the while realizing that I was stuck. I should have taken the time to buy the room online but just needed to end it all now. A very disappointing conclusion to an already tough day.

For a small but bright sideline, the restaurant manager was fantastic and gave me a great deal on a veggie burger and some extras. A few more things from the convenience store, but only the bare minimum, finished off the day, finally. A singular bad experience could not offset the more than a hundred times that my cycling motel visits had gone well, but still it would take a while for this one to fade into the past. I gladly closed the door and shut down the day.

Up early as always, I had thoughts of heading for New Mexico. Arizona had been fun, but I was excited to enter another state, especially since this was another one that I had never visited before. Leaving the Days Inn at Chambers was fine with me, but the room was definitely better than the hospitality of the office staff. I followed my Adventure Cycling map first thing in an effort to start the day on Route 66, beginning by crossing Interstate 40 and turning east. I was supposed to ride Route 66 on towards the next town. Less than a mile in, I came to a dead end and had to retrace my effort and rejoin the interstate again. Apparently, between the time that the map was printed and my visit, the road had been taken up and returned to pasture. I could tell where the road had been but now was no longer there.

Once I returned to my starting point, I faced east on the long entrance ramp and headed toward a fantastic sunrise on Interstate 40. A truck driver had even stopped his truck and was out taking pictures of it and we spoke briefly as I pedaled by. Again, I was in awe of God's power to set up such a spectacular show for both me and the driver on this Sunday morning.

Route 66 was going to be harder to track in New Mexico. California and Arizona had done a good job of posting signs. I noticed for the first time on the Adventure Cycling map the following statement: "Bicycle Route 66 does not always follow Historic Route 66." Several long side trips were available, and one of them included one of the oldest alignments of the famed road that was later abandoned.

This was a morning without a lot to see, but one thing did interest me. After beginning to ride one of the service roads that had also been Route 66, I saw signs for Fort Courage ahead. "F-Troop" was a favorite show of mine years ago, largely because of how funny it was but also because it was set during the Indian Wars and U.S. Army cavalry time following the Civil War. I absolutely am hooked on American history, and this was a segment of that history that has always intrigued me.

This Fort Courage looked a little like the setting for the TV show, especially the guard/lookout towers. But clearly, this roadside attraction long ago had its best day. Roof holes were not repaired, and no one appeared to take ownership, nor was there any reason for present day traffic to stop. It was just another former place of interest dying a slow death while the interstate traffic flashed by just yards away.

I entered Lupton near the Arizona and New Mexico line. Across the interstate was a huge rock formation with lots of holes in the walls and a sign that said Cliff Dwellers. Animal figures were on top of the cliff. A working truck stop was all around it, and some early morning traffic headed toward the Cliff Dwellers sign and the Yellowhorse Trading Post.

Now in New Mexico, I soon pedaled into the outskirts of Gallup. After riding the interstate for most of the morning, this was an occasion when all cyclists were directed off to rejoin the actual Route 66 as it headed into the downtown. Many times, the old route no longer existed until it connected to main travel roads that were also the high-traffic streets in the town or city where they remained in heavy use. Often, especially in the Southwestern towns, the central focus of the town itself remains on the sometimes 60-, 70- or 80-year-old roads that were Route 66 in one alignment or another.

Gallup had the largest number of motels of any town so far, some near the interstate and some downtown. I made a decision a couple of days before to spend the night at the El Rancho Hotel and Motel. Billboards had lined the interstate promoting the El Rancho, and my guidebook called it the "Gem of Gallup." For about 150 miles, I had seen the 1930s hotel described as combining the glory days of filmmaking and the Old West. Each billboard promoted another early film star who stayed at the hotel, often for days at a time. Some stars on the billboards included John Wayne, Clark Gable, Alan Ladd, Betty Hutton, Ronald Reagan, Jane Wyman and Jackie Cooper.

I passed by lots of motels, nearly all of them more reasonably priced than El Rancho. When I called the night before, I was told they had just a few rooms left. None of the other motels were very busy on this day, and I certainly seemed to pass them all as I pedaled toward El Rancho. It was easily the biggest and gaudiest hotel, but maybe not the best for present day. I walked in and found them expecting me, and check-in went very well until they had my charge card. I asked about the WiFi password but was told that the WiFi probably would not work unless I came to the lobby. The desk clerk encouraged me to use the hotel's restaurant, and I promised to check the menu. After seeing my room, the things that mattered to me were not up to par. No refrigerator, and the TV received just 10 channels. The furniture was worn and may have been around since Clark Gable. But when I arrived, lots of people were there, and the décor was a big plus. All around the upstairs over the lobby area, pictures of the early film stars were signed and filled just about every open space. I decided to make the best of it.

Not sure if it was OK to do so, I walked over into the original private room section of the hotel and found another surprise. Every door had the name of the famous star who had stayed there. Unable to see into the rooms, I walked the halls hoping that somebody would open their door, but no one did. Two different gatherings were going on in the hotel that afternoon, and both public ladies' restrooms were out of order and being worked on. Any woman who needed to use the bathroom was allowed to use the one in Gregory Peck's room, especially in the words of one patron, "After I complained enough!"

My idea was to use the long afternoon to look around Gallup, get some groceries and rest my legs a little. It was, after all, my first night in New Mexico, and I was in a hotel that was affectionately called "Hollywood Southwest." The good things about my room included a comfortable bed, although I was unlikely to find an uncomfortable one. I usually was so ready to fall asleep at night that I tossed about half a time and fell sleep before even turning once. The other good thing, which was always appreciated, was tremendous water pressure with plenty of hot water. An odd thing, even with the hot days, was that I liked to soak up a hot shower when time allowed.

The El Rancho would better serve its customers by updating things a little, and more of them might leave happy. But maybe they did anyway. It was cool to be among such history, but the motels all around it for half the price would have been an overall better deal. A good example was a very short restaurant menu and super high prices that included a grilled cheese sandwich for $9.30.

My food came from the nearby grocery store, and regardless of the disappointing accommodations, I slept well. Still, I was up even earlier than usual and ready to go. Since I had not replaced my flashing red light, it was safer to allow a few extra minutes to get a brighter sky. Well past the summer solstice now, the days were getting shorter.

Two options were available on this morning. I chose the one that most closely followed Route 66 even though most of the riding was on I-40. The other route, on the Adventure Cycling map, included plenty of off-route sight-seeing. I chose the direct route that included more heavy climbing over the Continental Divide and map information warning of very poor interstate shoulders.

On the way to Grants, I passed Fort Wingate, established in 1862 as a base for Kit Carson's campaigns against the Navaho Indians. Carson rounded up thousands and marched them 300 miles to Fort Sumner in what became known as "The Long Walk." The fort was moved to its present location in 1868.

Thoreau was the next town, and yes, it was named for author Henry David Thoreau. The Frontier Trophy Buckle Co., manufacturers of those oversized belt buckles awarded to rodeo champions, has its plant here.

Two more things happened as I rode toward Grants on a morning that was not quite as hot as recent mornings. I crossed over the Continental Divide with a climb that was not as bad as expected.

The official marker was off an exit road to the right of the interstate. I found the marker and was confident that any water that fell would now run downhill ahead of me.

Just past rejoining I-40, I thought my front tire was making an odd noise, and I watched it closely before determining that it was slowly going flat. I was near the top of the hill and was resigned to the fact that my first flat of the trip had just occurred. There was nothing to do but fix it, and I was glad that this flat was a front tire. Front tires are easy to drop off the frame and easy to put back. I leaned the bike against a reflector post and dropped out the front wheel just as I realized that fire ants were all over my feet. The bike sat on top of a big mound of them. Quickly, my focus turned to getting the ants off of me and moving the bike. My jumping around and slapping my feet with my hands had to look like a very strange dance indeed as the motorists drove by.

With that move accomplished, I laid the bike on the side and got my tools out and even took time to snack a little. Some leftover cookies hit the spot, and I began looking for the source of the flat. After taking the damaged tube out, I ran my fingers over the inside of the tire, searching for something sharp. Not one, but two pieces of steel belt from a truck tire had pierced the tire and the tube. I had to use a multi-tool to dig in and finally grab each piece separately before I could get them out. Then the new tube, slightly inflated, went into the tire and then the tire back on the rim. Then all of it went back on the frame, the tire by then fully inflated, and I jumped back on the road.

Another cyclist on a nice road bike pulled up beside me, and I met Nicholas Bloissa, on his way with another cyclist and a van to St. Augustine, Florida. Nicholas was fun to talk with, especially when I mentioned my just-repaired flat. He was also going to spend the night in Grants, and I wondered if I would see his group again once he rode away.

I had battled a fairly strong headwind on the way into Grants, and when I leaned the bike against a post, the wind blew it over. I had been in contact with Dr. Mac Bridges, a Grants resident whose mother lived back home in Salisbury. After calling Dr. Bridges, I headed on into town to find a motel and to stop by the visitors center and uranium mine. Santa Fe Avenue is the main drag where I stopped at the visitors center right away. The reconstructed New Mexico Mining Museum, part of the visitors center, was underneath the movie theater, and I took advantage of both. Both were very good, and I got some insight on how Grants got its start. The Grant brothers had a huge business in both ranching and mining, at one time employing as many as 4,000 men. Another reason for Grants' notoriety was that Elizabeth Taylor's husband, Mike Todd, was killed near here in a plane crash.

The Southwest Motel, with plenty of its own neon, was my home for the night. Another motel had done all the billboard advertising, but I stopped in here just to check the rate because the place's exterior had been kept up nicely. From the first contact with the owner, I was thrilled with everything about the motel. The best price of the trip, a nice room with everything I needed and a quiet environment were all I could ask for. I read reviews later that complained about the sound of the trains passing by across the street. Those trains were fine with me, and I never noticed them after I fell asleep. One special event occurred later as I was packing up to leave at about 5 a.m. the next morning. I went to the ice machine to fill my water bottles and no ice would come out. Before I got back to my room, the phone was ringing. The owner's wife, who I had not met previously, asked if she could help me. The ice machine had clogged overnight and with a little of her work, I soon had my ice.

But prior to that, I met Dr. Bridges, and we had a wonderful time at dinner. It was fun to share similar interests over the perfect meal. Mac's mom, Jeannie, had kept him posted on my ride from the start. We had a surprise at dinner, too. Nicholas, the cyclist on the way to St. Augustine, arrived at the same restaurant with his friend and the two ladies in their group. Nicholas looked so different in person without his helmet on that I didn't recognize him at first. Another brief but pleasant chat followed. Before dropping me off at the motel, Mac took me to Walmart for some groceries.

After such a fun time in Grants, one of my favorite towns along the way, I resumed the ride east on Route 66. Another new friend from Salisbury had let me know that I should go right by the Indian village of Paraje, her childhood home. Doreen May, a full-blooded Laguna Pueblo Indian, told me to look for a few things if I could take time to ride through Paraje. I knew from the first contact with Doreen that I would ride through her village because she made it sound so interesting. Route 66 did pass the village, so I made the turn into the streets to see it. Still early in the morning, not much was moving, although a few dogs checked me out. I rode to the top of the hill overlooking the village where the Catholic Mission Church sat as the dominant village structure for years.

According to a November, 8, 2014, article in Indian Country Today, more than two dozen federally recognized tribes live along Route 66. They are concentrated in Oklahoma, New Mexico and California. That article announced the launching of a partnership project involving tribes and the National Park Service called "American Indians and Route 66." One of the initiative's projects was to produce a guidebook to the American Indians along Route 66 in hopes of encouraging travelers to visit tribal destinations. The current cycling maps listed certain customs and rules without a lot of explanation, and I felt that this project would go a long way toward enhancing any cyclist's trip through these areas. I didn't see the guidebook available yet when I rode through.

Other Indian villages nearby were New Laguna and Laguna, and I pedaled through them while still on Route 66. I could see the interstate in the distance but enjoyed the close up look at the small towns of New Mexico. Route 66 was quite hilly until I eventually rejoined the interstate and heard Nicholas yelling from behind me as we topped a hill together. The view was so spectacular that we both stopped to enjoy it before moving on. Our conversation was about how God showed Himself as all powerful for having made the scenery so remarkable. We both counted ourselves as extremely fortunate to see all this from our bike seats.

A little later, I stopped at a McDonald's/truck stop combination for a breakfast deal. While taking a few minutes to eat, I noticed the local paper on one of the tables. Only the sports page remained, but one feature story caught my eye right away. Just brief mentions were made of baseball and NASCAR, but the local rodeo news dominated a couple of pages, most of it in this particular story. A local guy had qualified for the National Finals event coming up soon, and he said, "My horse is really excited and ready for this opportunity." I hoped to catch a rodeo later in this Route 66 adventure.

I saw Nicholas and his group again later in the day as we neared Albuquerque after a day of battling rolling hills — a couple of big ones — and a fierce headwind that eventually became a sidewind. Nothing affected my bike ride generally as much as the direction of the wind. That day was the perfect example that included the boost once the wind finally lessened and moved to the side. Pedaling just seemed to require so much less effort once the wind was less battering.

A bike shop in town was on my list as I headed into Albuquerque. With the heat building yet again, I entered the city limits with already 70 miles completed and with no idea what to expect when crossing the downtown area. A scenic panorama of the city below quickly led to a long downhill ride to the Rio Grande River before the payback climbing on the other side took place. Proving that Albuquerque was physically spread out, I had pedaled 12 miles within the city limits by the time I found the Two Wheel Drive Bike Shop, and I was still nowhere near the eastern edge of town. A quick stop at the bike shop for CO2 cartridges, a couple of tubes and a working red light didn't take long, and I got some ideas on places to eat and a grocery store.

Just a few blocks farther was another of the older choices for lodging, the Hiway House Motel. It was near the University of New Mexico campus and plenty of trendy shops, restaurants and college hangouts. After negotiating a lower rate than the desk clerk wanted to give me initially, I settled in for what I hoped would be a restful night. Serious climbing was on tap for the next day, but a very windy 82 miles was fine for this day. Other than a look around the Old Town area, I did not get a chance for sightseeing, but the long trip across town gave me a brief glimpse of a progressive city.

I found out later that Albuquerque has the nation's longest main street, called Central Avenue and lasting 18 miles from east to west. I also knew that I would be climbing nearly all day on the way to Santa Fe, much of the ride on a portion of the Route 66 alignment that was later abandoned.

Now roughly a third of my Route 66 ride was complete, and I was having a ball so far. In a few days, I planned to leave New Mexico and head east into Texas, yet another new state on a bike for me. The adventure continued!

CHAPTER 6

Riding uphill and across the last of New Mexico

A s I headed out of Albuquerque, I remembered the words of one of the bike shop guys there who told me that I was going to pedal uphill for a long time going east. At the time, I thought it could not be that bad. What followed was the closest I have been to a whole day of climbing. From the front door of the motel to the door of another one in Santa Fe, my maps showed a nearly steady incline.

My stay in the trendy area of Nob Hill had been pleasant except that the air conditioner struggled to keep up in the very large room. Ice cream opportunities were everywhere, and I was thankful for that. I did learn that Vivian Vance, Ethel Mertz of "I Love Lucy" fame, was born in Albuquerque.

My exit out the motel door came at an elevation of about 5,000 feet, and most of the early ride was a lower gear pull on more of Central Avenue. Sandia Mountain, the highest peak in the area, was ahead and getting closer. I had been advised by several contacts, including the Adventure Cycling map, "You absolutely must ride the Turquoise Trail!" So, I headed that way as the route for the day to Sante Fe.

On the way to the first town of Tijeras, I heard music coming from the side of the road in a spot with no houses and no visible people. My guidebook told me to be prepared to hear the music while I was climbing along for all I was worth. I read later that the music was "America the Beautiful," but I still was not sure exactly how it was provided.

On through Cedar Chest and into San Antonito on Route 14. I needed a boost because the climbing was very challenging, so I headed for a convenience store that might have egg and cheese biscuits. What I found was a brand new and exciting way for me to have breakfast. A burrito had never been an interesting choice for me, but in this store there was a lady making breakfast burritos to order. I looked over the choices and ordered an egg, cheese and potato burrito. Although it was obvious that most people want meat on their burrito, the smiling Hispanic lady made mine as a special order. It was huge and seemed to weigh a couple of pounds. I rode away from the store before trying it and had to ask directions at a confusing turn. Just after being sure I was on the right road, I stopped to eat half of the sandwich. It was so good that my legs felt great for the first time that day. The second half went back in my handlebar bag for a later boost. I was now a big fan of breakfast burritos.

Now riding on Route 14 and the Turquoise Trail, I headed for La Madera and then on to Golden. Nothing special seemed to be going on in Golden until I was about to leave it. Actually, leaving it and arriving happened within seconds of each other. The town was that small. Golden had room for the most interesting character of the whole trip who appeared beside the road and waved to me. Interesting and unusual both applied to Leroy Gonzalez, the self-proclaimed mayor of Golden. I stopped to take pictures of his place, which had a gold mine, cantina, teepee, fountain and a little enclosed shelter that looked like his place of residence. While I was taking pictures, Leroy invited me to come in for a tour, "Just five minutes is all I want. Everybody is in so much of a hurry that they won't stop to see what I have here."

Leroy did get a chance to take me on the tour, and I told him that five minutes was fine but that I had a long way to go. I was cautious when he took me inside the shelter but relaxed when he showed me all of the pictures that he had made of those who stopped by over the years. He had plenty of notes, too, thanking him for his hospitality. I watched as he hooked up the fountain and listened as he explained his huge dog and cat, both of dirt similar to sand art. Leroy wanted to know why I was riding the bike and not driving. After my explanation, he wanted to know why anyone would ever run so many miles. "Doesn't that just wear your body out sooner?" asked Leroy. After looking closely at his bottle collection, I bid Leroy goodbye and counted myself fortunate to have met a true Route 66 cycling adventure character. I don't know if Route 14 and the Turquoise Trail ever were part of Route 66, but Leroy would have been a welcome part of the entertainment of any driving journey. My five-minute stay turned in more than 20, and it was all fun.

The Turquoise Trail is about 45 miles long and takes the traveler through turquoise and coal mining country. Revived ghost towns along the way were Madrid, Golden and Cerillos. I had a spectacular view of the valley below as I rode through another section of high desert and flowering cactus, some red and some yellow.

Another surprise came next when I pedaled into Madrid. Right away, I noticed that people were everywhere around the buildings of the town as opposed to the abandoned look of most of the desert towns. Lots of the homes and other buildings were artistic shops of one form or another. I found a general store that also seemed to serve as an attorney's office. The clerk told me that Madrid had been a coal mining town that played out just after World War II. It had achieved a revival because of the amazing artisans who have chosen the place as home. I could have stayed all day and look forward to returning at a later date. A friend reminded me later in the day that

Madrid was the setting for Tim Allen's movie, "The Wild Hogs."

After Madrid came the time to keep my head down and pedal hard for Santa Fe, finally arriving at just after 3 p.m. My motel, another of the historic ones called the King's Rest Court Inn, was on the eastern side of town and meant a long ride uphill through lots of stop lights. Many of the motels that were built for the early alignment of Route 66 still remain. The King's Rest Court Inn was built in the 1930s and is the oldest in Santa Fe according to the owner. I loved the room, complete with its own carport, commode in a separate room from the rest of the bathroom and a ceiling made of logs and boards. The room was huge, quiet, clean and everything worked.

When I finally settled in for the night, I noticed that my shoes were wearing out on the sides and wondered if they would last the whole ride. My thigh muscles felt so strong, and I was confident that the remaining ride would go well.

After a great night's sleep, some uncertainty about my best route for the upcoming day remained. Some concern about the weather was heightened when I saw the forecast in the morning and a few minutes later saw the sky full of lightning even before the dark faded. Since I was a little off the Adventure Cycling map, I used a Mapquest printout to get back on track. Storms seemed all around me, but in the same manner as big-sky Montana, several cells could be seen off in the distance and none right overhead.

Leaving Santa Fe was a steady uphill push made more enjoyable by several rainbows off in the distance. Briefly, I rode on Canyon Road, said to have been an Indian footpath. My energy seemed to feed off the rainbows, and on I pedaled upwards. My goal for the end of the climb was Glorietta Pass, the highest point of all the Route 66 alignments. I was reminded that this version of Route 66 was pre-1937.

Glorietta Pass was famous for lots of other things, too. The early Indians, Spaniards and settlers passed through just like I did. The biggest surprise for me was that a small Civil War battle with major significance was fought here, too. I am a huge Civil War fanatic and read often on all the related subjects that I can. I have been to Gettysburg for the re-enactment of the July 1863 turning point of the Civil War. The results of that battle have been well known to even those of casual interest.

After my ride over the Glorietta Pass and finding a private roadside historical display, I had to find out more about the details of the battle called "Gettysburg of the West." Early in 1862, a Texas contingent of Confederate soldiers headed west to capture Santa Fe, New Mexico, and quickly did just that. Specific locations in Colorado and California were the targets of the force as it moved toward the pass. A Union detachment confronted the Rebels and engaged them in a two-day battle. The compelling Union victory caused the Rebel force to retreat and leave New Mexico. Had the invading force not been stopped, the riches of the west would have been wide open to the aspiring Confederacy.

The next town was Pecos, a small crossroads that was the gateway to Pecos National Historical Park. For the second time, I was able to tour a national park and use my park pass, although I had not thought of this before Santa Monica. A small museum detailed the history of the area, including the aforementioned Indians, Spaniards, settlers and the Civil War battle. The actual battle site was now in the park, but the focus of the national park was the ruins of two Spanish Mission churches that served the area from possibly the 1500s until the last was abandoned in 1838. The oldest pueblo ruins were once home to 2,000 residents. I took time to go on a walking tour of just over a mile that included several examples of the family residence of that time.

One small thing that I found interesting in this park was the constant signage that warned of rattlesnakes. Visitors were reminded not to approach the snakes and to report them to the staff. While I am a curious person at heart, no one ever needed to caution me about not approaching a rattlesnake. Thankfully, the only live rattlesnake that I saw on this whole trip was in a glass cage in a restaurant.

The heat was building rapidly as I left the park, and the only fluid I had was a tepid-tasting water from the national park. Nothing was exciting or refreshing about warm and tepid water, but it certainly beat the alternative. My riding for today was in an area listed on my maps as having limited services, this time for 96 miles. As a reminder, limited services meant that only a few points of supply for food and water, mechanical needs or accommodations would be available during this particular 96 miles of pedaling.

On this evening in what was called Romeroville, I was out of sorts a bit. I had the most unusual ride over the last 20 miles before making the campground where I would spend the night. There was some significant climbing, but it was broken by some downhill, too. Additionally, all within a two-hour period, I was just behind a motor home that came unhooked from the car that it was pulling, a car that evidently crossed the grass median and spun around on the opposite side of the interstate and some major paving work. The reason that I mentioned the paving work was because at least a few times in my long-distance cycling, paving work had been an issue. Once in the Grand Tetons of Wyoming, paving workers attempted to force me off the road in a move that would have negated the complete cross-country ride of summer 2013. I did not relent and finally convinced them to let me ride through the contested one mile of current paving work. This discussion and the ultimate approval to ride took about an hour on a near 100 degree day in July while we stood on new and very hot pavement.

This day's paving was being done on the eastbound side and was especially tight with barrels, trucks and still-steaming pavement, limiting the space for me to get through. Never sure exactly what I can do to take the bike through a construction area, I crossed the median to the other side of the interstate and walked across a bridge past the paving and then walked back across the median. Just as all of this was going on, two state trooper cars blasted by heading east. I knew they had bigger issues than me, so I got back on the bike and resumed my pedaling. Over another hill, I found the reason for the commotion. The car mentioned before had crashed into the opposite lanes and come to rest facing sideways. The driver, already in handcuffs, was being led away.

Back to the reason for being out of sorts. Bad weather was all around, some of it was expected to be severe, and I had just arrived in a campground. My iPad was having trouble connecting with WiFi, and my report back to the paper was in jeopardy. While warmly received at the campground, food choices were non-existent there. I bought some things at the nearby convenience store, remembering that I had no refrigerator and nothing but an optional bag of ice. The campground owner said that she was glad to sell me the bag of ice but she had nothing smaller. Drizzle and blustery winds had settled in the area, and at least one motor home entered the campground with the driver saying that the pouring rain was just down the road.

The KOA campground seemed to have shut down early, probably due to the weather issues. I walked around a little and found quite a few motor homes. Probably that was the reason that I had the campground bathroom to myself.

This had been a good day, significant for at least two reasons. The bike ride had been over a portion of Route 66 that also intertwined with the Santa Fe Trail and the Pecos Trail. Nearby, permanent wagon ruts left over from wagon trains headed west in the 1800s were visible in the baked mud at the Pecos National Park. Although travelers had crossed this area for hundreds of years, it still remained one of the most remote and finally abandoned parts of Route 66. This night turned out to be my only night in a campground on the whole trip. While still at near the highest point of elevation, I expected one of the coolest nights in recent memory. With my story finally completed and submitted, I turned in early as was my usual habit in campgrounds.

Sometime during the night, there was some more drizzle but no severe weather at all. It did get cooler and was one of the few times that I put on two shirts to ward off the chilliness of the early morning. I stopped by the convenience store, a quite good one, and picked up some food and water for the morning. It would be sometime this afternoon before I entered a town, and there was only one source of supplies listed, still close to 45 miles away.

After a short climb away from the store, I was back on Route 66 and headed more southeast than usual. It was cold enough that my hands were chilly, but the sun would eventually warm things once it got over the mountains. It took several hours for this to happen, and in the meantime I pedaled mostly downhill in vast, open-pasture countryside. Very few homes or buildings of any kind dotted the pastures, although it was unusual to see any cows. I did see plenty of working windmills near the road that provided water for what cows might have been out there. I may have mentioned before that I have a love affair with windmills, especially the old ones.

I knew where the store was supposed to be at about 45 miles into the morning and I planned to stop to reload on more water and a few more snacks. I came to the expected crossroads called Dilia and found the store, but it had been closed for quite a while. It was actually a bar that advertised groceries and snack items. At this point, I had some food still left over and water, too. I just pedaled on past, feeling just fine about it, even though I knew that it would now be a total of 60 miles of riding before I saw another store. Normally, I enjoyed telling about the towns that I pass through but today there was nothing of that sort to tell so far.

My goal was to spend the night in Santa Rosa, a busy little Route 66 town that had some interesting points. After days of extremely dry desert and hot temperatures, Santa Rosa was such a change! One of the first things that I noticed was a huge downtown lake in their community park. Already, I knew of the popular Blue Hole and wanted to see it. Riding past the lake, I followed the signs and a good portion of the traffic to another Parks and Recreation parking area. The sign had the prices for parking but cyclists were all admitted free, even though I had my best excuses ready to avoid paying.

The Blue Hole is 80 feet deep and 60 feet wide with deep blue, chilly water. The year-round water temperature remains in the low 60s and seemed perfect for this very warm day. Two lifeguards monitored the dozens of swimmers, paying special attention to a rock-diving platform. It was certainly an unusual attraction that swimmers used all year and was a popular site for SCUBA diving practice, too. Once I saw the place, I realized that no other water sources in the area were likely to have been as interesting as the Blue Hole. A packed parking lot during an early afternoon supported this statement.

Santa Rosa, nicknamed the City of Natural Lakes, was already becoming a favorite. I had watched the swimmers and some of those reluctant to jump in the deep Blue Hole for a short time, then headed on back to town in search of a motel room. Back on Route 66, motels were abundant and so were restaurants and other businesses. I found the singular steepest hill in the center of an otherwise non-hilly town that I have seen. It was so steep that I struggled mightily to make it to the top and realized that I already had started to pedal away from town. Interstate 40 was hustling by when I topped the hill finally and continued to look for my motel.

I had called ahead and reserved a room at the La Mesa Motel, another one of the older ones. Just before the climb up the big hill, I crossed the Pecos River for the third time in the last few days. There was more water close by than I had seen in the past two weeks. In fact, the Pecos probably had something to do with eroding out the bottom of the just-climbed hill. Coronado and his Spanish force had crossed the Pecos here in 1541. Old West jargon used to include by manner of direction, the saying of "East of the Pecos," or "West of the Pecos." While most references came from much farther from the river, Santa Rosa residents could have done the same as the river split the town.

The motel appeared on my left, and I was surprised that it looked like a neat and newer motel. I rode into the parking lot and found the office closed but quickly spotted the maid outside one of the rooms. She told me that she would get the owner's daughter and have her come to let me in my room. The La Mesa just had the feeling of a good place, and for once, I calmly waited until she drove in.

After just a few minutes, I was squared away in what I found was the newer section that connected with the renovated older section of the motel. A newer room within a historic motel worked well, especially with the beautiful neon sign out front. A reader emailed me to make sure to visit the Route 66 Auto Museum, which just happened to be less than a mile past the motel.

Just before leaving the room for the museum visit, I got a message from Salisbury resident Lauren Martz by email. Lauren, a geology intern who was working in the Santa Fe area, had been following my trip along with her parents. We planned to meet later in the afternoon, 2,000 miles from home.

The museum, the best car museum of the ones I heard about, was fantastic. With no real hurry, I took the time to slowly make my rounds of about 30 cars and walls full of memorabilia. There was a small snack bar and a gift shop, while every bit of the museum was so much fun. The nostalgic place with Elvis and Marilyn cutouts and 1950s music evoked memories of my friends who had owned some of the same cars on display here. My own 1966 Mustang of those high school years was also long gone, but for just a few moments, I wished that it was not. I wonder how many of my friends might have thought the same way, especially after touring such a quality museum with current car values posted prominently. The revolving display of vehicles included a 1939 Dodge Business Coupe, A 1947 COE (cab over engine) pickup truck and a 1957 Chevy Bel Air convertible.

The eastern end of Santa Rosa, near the museum, had several large convenience stores so I stopped in briefly to add to my food reserves. I had passed the town's grocery store earlier on the other side of the big hill and decided to eat what I could find without climbing that monster again.

Shortly afterwards, I was back at the motel and met the owner. He filled me in on the history of how his family acquired the 1940s La Mesa and how the renovations had come about. In fact, I walked up on part of the family as they discussed another renovation. During this conversation, Lauren drove into the parking lot. She was a bright and funny person, and I really enjoyed visiting with her. Lauren knew that her mom and dad would read my report on that day's happenings and would be surprised to see she had visited. We laughed, and I contacted nighttime copy editor Andy Mooney back at the Salisbury Post and told him what had happened. We all agreed that Andy would try to get my picture with Lauren in the paper the next morning. Lauren left and headed back to Santa Fe after a very nice visit. I was confident that she was going to be successful at geology and whatever else she plans.

My cellphone didn't work that day for the first time on the trip, and I hoped the reception would return soon once I headed east the next day. After 67 miles completed that day in the longest isolated stretch so far associated with Route 66, more wide open spaces were on tap for at least the next day until I reached Tucumcari. Santa Rosa made my list of favorite towns easily and I went to bed looking forward to leaving New Mexico soon. I felt great, knowing that I had been treated well here at the La Mesa by the staff — so well that for the first time, I overslept by about 20 minutes.

By hustling, I still hit the road at 5:30 a.m., about as early as I could based on the available light. Interstate 40 was close by, and I jumped on it in the cool morning air while wearing two shirts once again. The second one didn't last long. The first town of the morning was Cuervo, a sort of ghost town along the interstate. Most of the buildings were in poor repair, although one picturesque old church still had someone caring for it. It was another example of a small town left behind when the super slab replaced Route 66.

My maps called for following Route 66 from this point, but I quickly found that the road was not consistently in good shape. Some portions were rough, and the road even had grass growing through it. After finding a portion blocked, I gladly got back on the interstate, which was again running parallel with the old highway. Once back on the interstate, I saw that the Route 66/frontage road soon disappeared completely. Newkirk was the next crossroads, and the one store there showed no activity as I passed by. I was headed for Tucumcari, one of the towns that seemed to be a "can't miss" for an interesting visit.

Purposely, I did not have a plan about how far I would go on this day. One of the most fun things for me was to let the day unfold as it would, with no real limits. With that, I knew that Tucumcari had some points of interest and some of the most marketed motels on Route 66. It seemed right to go there and just figure it out.

Entering Tucumcari on an interesting part of Route 66, I rode on a wide, four-lane road with abandoned motels and a truck stop that must all have been loaded with traffic at one time. There had been no harsh climbing all morning, and a tremendous tailwind had developed during the late morning. Just before noon, I rode into the main part of town and decided to visit the Tucumcari Historical Museum. I had read reviews about this museum that suggested that no visitor should miss it and that it was loaded with history.

Museum Director Paula Neese met me at the door, and I was immediately immersed in a friendly conversation with her and two volunteers. One was Paula's husband, Donnie, who told me that the old building had been a hospital, a school and was even used for World War II glider training, among other things. I had already seen from outside that the grounds were crowded with interesting displays including a huge wooden windmill and a Vietnam-era fighter jet. For a nominal fee, I toured multiple buildings crammed full of historical items. Cowboy and ranching displays, including an actual cattle drive section, got me hooked on the place right away. There were more exhibits on ranching, railroading and just everyday life in Tucumcari during various eras. Paula and Donnie might just get another visit from me in a few years, and there is no doubt that I will see things that I missed this time. Before I left, Paula gave me something special to help with any rattlesnake encounter that I might yet have. I left with actual rattlers from the tail of a snake who probably didn't want to give them up. Paula told me that other rattlesnakes would leave me alone if I shook my very own rattlers at them. Only as a last resort!

With the strong tailwind blowing, I was tempted to keep riding east, but after some thought and a further conversation with Paula and Donnie, I decided to see if I could get a reasonable motel for an afternoon of sightseeing. A sign near the first exit for Tucumcari off I-40 said that the town had 34 motels. I think that most of that number remained, and Paula suggested a few of them.

The motel search in itself became interesting even though I had already ruled out the Blue Swallow, possibly the most famous motel on all of Route 66. I emailed them the night before and found no vacancy. Paula told me that a full house was normal for the Blue Swallow. The outside was decorated in such a wonderful way with classic cars, swings and flowers that looked fantastic. I headed to the Safari Motel, where the owner told me that the office was closed and would not reopen for at least an hour. Not the most hospitable answer, and it seemed to be my prompt to head on toward other options. Next, I leaned my bike against the overhang of the office of another motel and tried the door. About that time, I saw that owner walking towards me and warmly asked how she could help. I inquired about a room and then quickly realized that these rooms were out of my price range. The owner sent me down the street to what turned out to be the find of the day when I entered the Historic Route 66 Motel, one of several individually owned motels by the same name along the famous highway.

While I have to be conscious of keeping the costs low for daily expenses to be a good steward of my sponsorships, the motel search has been a game that I love to play just about every day. Because I don't always win the game, the days that I do become even more special. The Historic Route 66 Motel in Tucumcari was just one of the days when I hit the jackpot. The motel itself had everything I needed plus a few special add-ons that made the visit unique. Another of the older motels, but one obviously managed with care, the 66 Motel hit the spot for me. An extra large and nicely deco-rated room, a big bed, nice refrigerator, shower, TV and microwave filled my list of desires, but these were not all that the motel had to offer. Two older trainer airplanes, one with the back sawed off so it looked as if the rest was inside the building, were part of the uniqueness. Large outdoor chairs just outside my room made sit-ting there very comfortable. Most people might find the fact that I love spending time watching traffic go by from a nice chair at the end of the day a big surprise. After all, I usually spend the whole day in traffic. However, from a nice chair with a cold drink in my hand, nothing was better to help me unwind and relax. Addition-ally, this 66 Motel had '50s and '60s music playing softly outside the rooms. A wonderful and helpful owner topped off one of the best motels I had ever visited.

Once settled, I biked back against the wind to the Mesalands Dinosaur Museum and toured it. Dinosaur fossils have been found all over the area, and the Mesa Technical College remained involved in further study. Real-size dinosaur models were very interesting to see as was all the information about their lives and habitat. I also stopped by the grocery store and visited with a mom and her kids who wanted to know about my bike ride. I could never do enough of this and often wondered if maybe, just maybe, one or two of these kids might someday enjoy seeing the country by bicycle as I have.

I continued to struggle with both my iPad and cellphone, nei-ther of them working correctly. My story and pictures finally trans-mitted back to the paper, but it was touch and go for a while. The cellphone still showed no service. I hoped to get both working cor-rectly by tomorrow.

With an easy distance of just 65 miles, I was happy with the day and especially the visit to Tucumcari. One of my goals throughout all four of my summertime rides has been to visit a rodeo along the way. A junior rodeo was in fact happening in Tucumcari when I entered town and it continued on into this night. I had my chance, but passed it up because of the distance from the motel and the late start for the nighttime portion of the rodeo.

While riding around town, I saw Tee Pee Curios, a 1940s gas station that was famous with Route 66ers. There also was a sombrero-shaped Mexican Restaurant and dozens of colorful murals about town. Many of the murals had something to celebrate the Route 66 theme.

I enjoyed hearing the fable about how the town got its name. One version said that an Indian maiden named Kari was so grieved over the death of her lover, Tocom, that she took her own life. Her father, upon discovering the tragedy, said, "Tocom! Kari!" Or another similar word, kamukari, is Comanche for ambush, so feel free to take your choice. The first certainly had more mystique and appeal to me.

The time had come to leave New Mexico and head into Texas! Is it possible to have more fun than I was having right now? The halfway point was near, so much more adventure lay ahead.

CHAPTER (7)

Texas first, celebratory pie and then Oklahoma

Another new day and more adventure on the horizon has an incredible ability to recharge my batteries. Many times, I have gone to bed on the road bone tired. Once in a while, I have thought that this next particular day might be a good one for rest. But always, the first thoughts on awakening have been full of energy and excitement about the upcoming day. Any possibility of a layover has gone out the door with me right behind it on the bike as the journey continued.

My stay at the Historic Route 66 Motel had been wonderful. Cathy Fulton and her motel were all that I could ask for. Tucumcari had been fun for an afternoon and evening, but now it was time to ride, experience and discover. I rode out of town on Route 66 on another of those days that I couldn't wait to get underway.

With points of supply about every 15 to 20 miles, any shortage of available food and water had eased somewhat. I passed through crossroads or towns called San Jon, Bard and Endee before crossing into Texas in Glenrio, a ghost town which sits on the Texas-New Mexico border. Most of the scenery was rangeland with very few trees and even fewer visible cows.

After I entered Texas, I was suddenly able to ride on a section of Route 66 near Glenrio that was in great shape. After a long climb, I found a completely new environment with green row crops and pastures. The horizon was dotted with massive windmill generators, the same as I found in Canada the previous year. Glenrio was featured in the 1938 movie "The Grapes of Wrath," based on the book by John Steinbeck.

About midday on a beautiful Sunday, I rode into Adrian, Texas, the celebrated midpoint of the most recent alignment of Route 66. Some of the older versions of the famous highway, such as the Santa Fe section, were no longer included in this midpoint mileage estimate. Regardless, Adrian was significant, and I thought it worthwhile to visit the famous Midpoint Café for some of the vaunted pie. Not normally a pie eater, it just felt proper to stop in and make my own celebratory statement.

Of course, I wanted Elvis Pie made with bananas, peanut butter and chocolate. My own favorite pie is pecan and I got a slice of that, too. I read that when the café first started making pies, they messed up the crusts and some called them "ugly." Now carrying the Midpoint's trademark ugly crust-style pie, I had to make room in my bags with plans to eat it once the day's ride was completed.

The slogan of the Midpoint Café is, "When you are here, you are halfway there!" The most widely recognized total distance of the current Route 66 was 2,448 miles. But again, certain parts of the older alignments were not included.

While waiting for my pie, I talked with the manager of the café about the area. He told me that there were only 166 listed residents in Adrian but that there were about 28,000 cows in the nearby feedlots at any time. I also read that the reason for all the windmills and windmill generators was because the Amarillo area is considered the windiest in the U.S. I had already ridden for 15 miles of good Route 66 road with endless windmill generators. This was the first time that I had seen an extended section of newly paved Route 66 with nice-looking Route 66 logos. Each state has placed its own name on them, too. I hoped that Texas would be good stewards of the road, similar to what Arizona had done.

Still lightly traveled on this Sunday afternoon, the good road made for an easy ride into Vega. I quickly spotted an older Route 66 motel that had a very good price but I thought had problems with its WiFi. We tried a couple of locations, and my iPad wouldn't connect, not even in the office. The owner even called his son, their IT guy, for advice. We couldn't make it work, so I told him that I would ride around the town a little bit and might come back. Next, I called a chain motel and asked for their rate for a long distance cyclist. The reply was quite high, and I reminded her that I was on a bicycle and might have as many as 40 nights on the road. She didn't budge, so I headed out toward the interstate and spotted a Days Inn that had a Dairy Queen close by and a huge convenience store across the road, so I went inside to check the rate. Once the manager spotted my bike, I didn't even have to ask for his best rate. We talked briefly about my ride, and I was soon settled in a room too nice for me and too reasonably priced for the Fourth of July weekend after 77 miles for the day.

More focused on the pie in my bags and the DQ next door than I should have been, food was my immediate need. As soon as I rolled my bike into the room, I attacked the Elvis pie, a huge slice that was almost enough to ease my hunger for a few minutes. That pie was so good that I had to eat the pecan slice, too.

After the pie, I felt great except for one thing. My cellphone had started working earlier that day, but my WiFi issues that had continued since the campground in Romeroville still had not improved. I knew from past overnights in a Days Inn that their WiFi usually works great, and often they do not require a password. Yet, here in Vega, I couldn't get connected at all. I kept trying and even asked the manager if there had been any complaints, to which he replied that there had not.

I even considered calling customer service for Apple or Verizon, the carrier for just my iPad. Then I remembered what a teenager at a motel had told me a couple years earlier somewhere along the Atlantic coast. He said that there was a soft reset, but I didn't remember what he did. With my phone now working, I Googled how to do it and within about five minutes had solved the problem. Now, it really was a good day! Dairy Queen was next. For a day that started with no real plan, I couldn't be happier with how it turned out.

My beard continued to grow, and my earlier pledge of shaving when I reached the end of the desert was on my mind. The edge of the desert was close, but the beard was easy to keep and people had remarked several times that they liked it. Honestly, I did too, at least for the time being. I didn't shave that night.

When I think of Texas, Amarillo comes to mind as the prettiest name for a town as well as the subject of George Straight's hit song, "Amarillo by Morning." Most people would think that a guy who was averaging five to six hours of sleep a night would not want to get up early. For whatever reason, the more excited I am, the earlier I have to get up. Excitement crept into my sleep, and I was awake earlier than planned. I was up and ready to go while the sky was still pitch dark the next morning.

A trip across the street to get some food for my bags and an egg and cheese biscuit for breakfast took some time, but not enough. With my flashing light working well, I decided to go ahead and ride in the dark. Already aware that the road was freshly paved, I wasn't worried about holes and I knew that traffic was minimal. All the cars and trucks headed for the interstate, and I pedaled toward Route 66.

Before leaving town, I saw a bright falling star and two foxes that crossed the road just ahead of me. Just after that, a skunk started to cross but turned back. From that point on, I knew that the ingredients were in place to make this a special day.

It was a chilly morning, one of the coolest that I experienced throughout the ride. My hands were cold enough that I wished for a thin pair of gloves. Despite that, still in the dark, I felt great physically. The road was smooth and nearly flat, so flat that I could see the remains of a thunderstorm ahead of me with lightning illuminating the high clouds. Off to the left, miles and miles of the wind generators were doing their work, easily identifiable by the red flashing light on the nose of each one. Amazing to me, those red lights for as far as I could see all flashed in unison.

As I rode ahead, meeting only two cars in the first ten miles, all of the visual effects were a sort of sensory overload as the sky began to brighten. The clouds were purple and maroon as they parted enough to see the sun make its appearance. Tears came to my eyes as I tried to accept this amazing demonstration of God's power, assuring me that I was safe in His hands. By this time, I counted this morning as the best early morning ride of my experience. Throughout the morning's ride, I sang as much as I could remember of "Amarillo by Morning."

By this time, Route 66 was one of the frontage roads for Interstate 40. I realized how enjoyable it was to ride with the big rigs and other traffic probably 30-50 feet away but with no worries of watching for the interstate trash that flattened a bike tire so easily. While riding, I liked plenty of scenery and especially enjoyed big trucks and billboards.

The next town was Wildorado, beginning a stretch of flat plains that looked much like Kansas. Huge combines sat at the edge of wheat fields that they had harvested, probably waiting for another season of soybean harvests. I noticed the burned-out motel the manager at the Midway Café told me about.

I rode on to Bushland, now having pedaled 18 early morning

miles during which I only met two cars. On this Fourth of July that felt like a Sunday but wasn't, I stopped at a nice convenience store that had a small deli and two welcoming clerks. My needs were simple: a breakfast of some kind and directions to Cadillac Ranch. Right away, I found another of the egg, cheese and potato breakfast burritos. When I paid for it, I asked about how to find the roadside attraction with a row of older Cadillacs buried nose first in a cornfield. The clerk told me to keep riding for about four miles and I couldn't miss it. Oddly, my cycling map didn't say where to find them, but mentioned the big draw.

I rode ahead and found the site with already about 100 Route 66 enthusiasts in the corn field. The common practice for years had been to bring a can of spray paint or pick up one off the ground and lend an artistic contribution of some kind. The thunderstorms of the night before had most of the cars surrounded in standing water, but still the painting went on. I watched a few people who searched through the hundreds of cans left behind for one with any paint still in it. I noticed a foreign family of four that arrived in a beautiful 1960s Cadillac convertible, already with the top down.

Cadillac Ranch was a grouping of ten Cadillacs, vintage 1949 to 1963, that was originally placed in a wheat field as an art exhibit. At an average cost of about $200, most of the cars came from junk yards. The cars were planted at an angle that corresponded with the angle of the Great Pyramid in Egypt. They were placed in 1974 by the art group Ant Farm and funded by millionaire Stanley Marsh as sort of an evolution of the grand Cadillac of its time and as alternative and interpretive art. In 1997, the cars were quietly unearthed and moved close to Interstate 40 to get them away from the growing city of Amarillo. The cars were briefly restored to their original colors by the Hampton Inn chain, but the restoration lasted less than 24 hours. Visitors were then encouraged to write graffiti and spray paint the cars. This was certainly one of my favorite sites along the way, a site that Marsh once called "the Stonehenge of America."

Amarillo, now a city of nearly 200,000 people, was my next stop. I followed Route 66 through town rather easily with no traffic hassles, possibly influenced by the holiday off for most drivers. The big helium plant that supplied as much as 95 percent of the world's supply until after World War II sat on the right as I passed. A large percentage of today's helium still comes from the Amarillo area.

With one of the longest continuous streams of billboards I have seen, the Big Texan Steak Ranch attracted me enough to find the place, although I had to cross the interstate to get there. Those billboards had advertised the place for the last 600 miles, touting the restaurant, motel, blacksmith shop, gift shop and the biggest steak dinner I had ever heard of. Since 1960, the restaurant had offered a 72-ounce steak dinner with all the fixings free to anyone who could eat it all. The signs said that thousands had tried but only a small percentage had been able to consume all the food. Not only do they keep up with who has eaten the food, but also how long it took them. One person, a 125-pound woman, consumed everything in just four minutes and has remained the grand champion for years.

I rode through downtown Amarillo before leaving and then headed out of town on Route 66. The road continued to be good as I passed through Conway, not much more than a crossroads, and on to Groom where I would spend the night. The high temperatures were now back to around 100, and I was just about roasted at the end of 84 miles for the day.

Groom had about 500 residents, but the signs of its prosperity years ago were still evident. A wide four-lane road travels through town that has very little traffic now. What I did find were two convenience stores, a decent motel, lots of huge grain elevators, a giant cross and another Dairy Queen. The giant cross was at a rest area on Interstate 40 and was 190 feet tall. Lit at night, it was as tall as the giant wind generators and was touted as the tallest cross in the Western Hemisphere.

Generally, past the lesser populated areas, I was able to get by with carrying less food and water. I had a tailwind all day and decent roads but less interaction than usual with people. Usually, when I didn't get to meet people on one day, the next one turned out to have lots of interaction.

The Dairy Queen and one of the convenience stores were next to my motel. Two visits to the Dairy Queen, once for a large and once for a medium pineapple milkshake, now recorded as my first double header, closed out the best day so far on the Route 66 adventure. I already couldn't wait to go out the door again.

Storms were around again when I got ready to leave the Chalet Motel in Groom the next morning. The predicted high for the day was 99, and I wanted to leave as early as possible, but the darkness lingered so long that I missed out on a daylight viewing of Groom's leaning water tower. A popular sight along Route 66, the water tower was actually built that way as a conversation piece.

I watched this morning's thunderstorm doing its thing about ten miles ahead. There was more lightning than yesterday morning, but the storm seemed to have taken the wind away, even causing the giant wind generators to sit still. This was the only time that I saw them not turning, which I should have taken as a sign that something odd was about to happen with the wind.

The next town was Alanreed, a strange and quirky little place. Most of the current town consisted of abandoned buildings and one nicely restored 66 Super Service Station. Originally, the town was called Eldridge, but when the railroad came through, the whole town packed up and moved to be near it. Before the town settled on the name of Alanreed, it was called Prairie Dog Town, Spring Tank and Gouge Eye which had something to do with a barroom brawl.

McLean was the next town, another town with one-way streets a block apart left over from the heyday of Route 66. I rode both the eastbound and westbound sides and found another wonderfully restored old Phillips 66 service station and then a small restaurant called Lollie's Diner where, after some thought, I stopped in for breakfast biscuits. I noticed that the diner seemed to serve as a small emergency grocery store, as well. I ordered a couple of breakfast biscuits, hoping to talk to the waitress a little about McLean, but she seemed uninterested in talking either to me or the one other customer. Lollie was in the back making the biscuits, so I never spoke to her. I did receive a brief nod from the customer. After all this, I just took the biscuits and ate one on the sidewalk in the shade and the other on the road later. On the way out of town, I noticed the "Devil's Rope" Museum, another name for barbed wire.

As the weather got hotter, the next town was Shamrock. I needed some ice and cold liquids and headed for a convenience store. Shamrock seemed to be doing pretty well and was proud of its Route 66 heritage with lots of older motels and the Chamber of Commerce located in a fantastically restored gas station called the U Drop Inn.

The wind was really howling from the south now, a harsh sidewind that had only a minor positive of slight cooling. The heat and this wind, along with some hills, made this afternoon more challenging than most. With just 21 miles left for the day, I just kept pedaling and was soon looking for the Welcome to Oklahoma sign. I remained on Route 66, but still next to the interstate. When there was not a sign on Route 66, I doubled back and rode on the interstate just long enough to get my desired picture of the state sign. I had never been to Oklahoma at all, and certainly this was my first visit on a bike, so the sign was important.

Texola was the first town in Oklahoma, and it was not appealing. Everything looked abandoned, with the existing population listed at 36. I knew ahead of time that a highlight would be the one-cell jail, and it was easy to find. Not a person seemed to be moving as I leaned my bike against the outside wall and walked in for a look around. Pictures of criminals who had been hanged and one who was beheaded were on the walls, although it was unclear how many of these bad guys might have been incarcerated in this jail.

Still on 66, I pedaled the long and lonely road to Erich. At one time, this was a bustling road with two lanes on each side. Over time, the two westbound lanes had deteriorated quite a bit. My eastbound side was not great, and several times I wondered if I was still on the right road. Gradually, the road got more traffic and once Business I-40 joined it, I didn't worry about being off course. The quality of the road improved, too.

About parched from the heat and the ever-present wind, I rode into Erich and immediately noticed that one of the recommended motels was closed. I was on Roger Miller Boulevard and followed it until a stoplight came into view, stopping at a convenience store for liquids and ice. Two very nice clerks told me about the available motels and what else was in town. Erich has about 1,000 residents with a small grocery, downtown section and the one stoplight as far as I could tell. Besides Roger Miller Boulevard, named after the famous singer, the other road crossing the town square was named after Sheb Wooley. Wooley was also a country musician but gained fame later for his long-running part on the TV series "Rawhide."

My destination was the Days Inn. With good luck there recently, I headed that way and found it right across from a huge Love's Truck Stop. No Dairy Queen in site, but I couldn't expect that every day. Those large truck stops were well stocked, often now with healthy snacks, and I was excited about only a short walk to get my food. Maybe I sounded then like the person who drives around to find the nearest parking space before going to work out at the YMCA.

After part of one day in Oklahoma, I had noticed how much Oklahoma looks like home in North Carolina. There is green grass and trees, with both getting more viable as I progressed farther east. A punishing day of 80 miles was fine with me, and my hope was that the wind would abate somewhat tomorrow. I knew that the temperature would not.

I had a wonderful and very restful night at the Days Inn, and the food choices were varied at the truck stop. Fruit cups, especially those with watermelon, were perfect, and a nice Subway sandwich was a treat, too. One of the things that I did in the evening if possible was continuous eating along with plenty of hydration — so much so that I have a huge amount of trash by bedtime. I always took pride in myself for keeping a motel room or a campsite as clean as I could, often close to the way I found it. A big plastic bag was usually filled about to the brim with everything I have discarded, and I wondered if the motel staff wouldn't think that five people used the room. But then they would look at the bed and see that it was hardly used, leaving them to think further that it must have been a huge guy with an eating disorder who stayed here.

Once again, I took a chance and rode out in the dark. I stayed on the same road to retrace my path back to the one stoplight of downtown Erich while no traffic made riding easy, especially with my new flashing light that worked so well. With a cloudy dawn, it was nice to have only one vehicle that met me in the first 13 miles. Mostly flat riding on more of Route 66 that had decayed still made for a quick trip to Sayre and an unexpected McDonald's on the edge of town. Usually, the McDonald's and other chain restaurants were in high-traffic areas, but this one was in a much quieter part of town.

I ordered my usual Egg McMuffins, two for a better deal, and an order of hotcakes. As one of two customers, Caren took my order and asked me if I would do a survey while I ate. If I did, then she promised to set me up with plenty of coupons for the next several days. Always in a hurry to eat breakfast and then take advantage of the cooler and less windy morning, I still took time to do the survey. In the meantime, another customer came in and she got that person to do the same.

Finished with breakfast, or just the hotcakes and one Egg Mc-Muffin with the ham removed, I took my completed survey back to the counter with big expectations. Caren took out a stack of "free coffee" coupons and started to hand them to me. I declined them, since I have never been a coffee drinker. She had more coupons for fries and burgers. I took a few for the fries and had to be happy with that.

Sayre was a nice little town with beautiful parks and clean streets. I rode the edge of town for a while and found a softball complex with a permanent rodeo arena. The more I pedaled east, the more Oklahoma had a North Carolina look. People had nice yards, and they don't fence them in. From California though Arizona and New Mexico, nearly every homeowner had his yard fenced in or at least a gate to the driveway. Fences were less common in Texas and then almost non-existent in Oklahoma.

Making good time for the morning, I rode on to Elk City, a town of about 12,000 that sets the bar pretty high. One primary attraction that I planned to visit was a whole city block of museums centered around the National Route 66 Museum. The wind was building quickly along with the temperature as I pedaled into the parking lot. One price was good for at least three museums that I planned to visit and another, focusing more on the Elk City area, that I didn't.

The National Route 66 Museum was as good as promised with lots of vehicles, recorded thoughts from those who traveled America's Highway, and plenty of memorabilia that showed how much fun could have been had on the road. Another museum was all about the farming and ranching that was a mainstay of Oklahoma. Yet another was a long series of storefronts that depicted how an early 20th century town might have looked. This was another place that made my list to visit again.

Back on the bike, I battled the wind past small Canute and soon arrived in Clinton on Route 66. A pattern had now emerged that Business 40 would peel off the main interstate and join with Route 66 through the downtown area before rejoining the main interstate. Clinton had more museums, but my focus was on the Tradewinds Motel. I had a read a few days before that Elvis Presley had stayed multiple times in this motel, all in room 215. Right away, I found the motel and quickly spotted the famous room. Usually, I am OK to stay in not-the-nicest room, especially if I get to offset that with a great price. The building, actually a larger motel than I expected, looked terrible. Doors looked like they had been broken into and quickly repaired. The curtains inside the rooms looked mismatched and sometimes torn. Possessions sat near the doors of the rooms, a sure sign that some of the rooms were long-term residences.

I was especially hot that afternoon and thought that the wind played a big part in that. When I mentioned the motel at a nearby store, several of the store employees advised against staying there by going into explicit detail, so I didn't.

Leaning toward finding a room elsewhere, I asked Barbara from Clinton if Weatherford, the next town, had Route 66 motels. Having heard my conversation with the store clerk, she agreed with the decision to move on and told me how to continue across town and rejoin Interstate 40. She said I would be happy with Weatherford.

Arriving at the edge of town after a huge climb out of Clinton, I noticed a sign near the city limits that lauded Weatherford as one of the 10 fastest-growing towns, but I wasn't sure if that meant in Oklahoma or the United States. I made a good deal on a quiet motel on Main Street/Route 66 and was glad to finally get out of the wind. Gusts of 30-40 mph continued through the afternoon, sometimes pushing me quickly sideways. It was odd to ride with a sideways lean into the wind while riding straight ahead. Back-to-back days of this wind had been tiring, for sure. The wind generators had returned, and this time they had plenty of work with the howling gusts.

Route 66 had become spotty. The maps called for me to ride certain sections of it, again mostly along the frontage roads. Today, more than any sections previously, Route 66 seemed to be there at times and then suddenly gone. Once when the road became rough and spotty, I got back on the interstate while keeping my eye on what happened to the frontage road. Suddenly it came to a stop with a barrier in place, and only a dirt road remained that headed out over a hill to the south. Barbara from Clinton had warned me to expect a good bit of this for the next several days.

Once in my room with the air conditioner turned on high, I headed across the street to a wonderful place called Braum's. With an almost full-fledged ice cream shop and a small fresh-market grocery, I was in heaven. Disappointed that Braum's didn't carry pineapple milkshakes, I ordered an extra large strawberry one and picked up the rest of my food in the grocery section. It was easy to love this place and as the ride continued, the Braum's chain got my ice cream business several times.

The forecast for my ride into the Oklahoma City area was even worse as I found out that evening. I woke from a good sleep at the

Scottish Inn in Weatherford with the winds already blowing at 18 mph, very high for so early in the morning. This was a fun town to visit and seemed to be doing just fine. I enjoyed the ride out of town while looking around at the early morning openings of some of the restaurants. Already, I was hungry but kept pedaling because another challenging day was expected.

Route 66 went missing in several areas again, so I ended up riding on the interstate, especially since there were no towns for the first 30 miles of the morning's cycling. My early objective was Fort Reno, just before the town of El Reno. Back on Route 66, I pedaled to the entrance to Fort Reno and saw that I had a long ride with the wind blowing fiercely behind my bike — good for the time being, but worrisome for the ride out later.

Fort Reno was established in 1874 as a military camp to aid in the Indian Wars. Troops from Fort Reno preserved the peace and directed the orderly transition from Indian territory to individual farms and ranches. The fort was also a quartermaster depot to other forts farther west. During World Wars I and II, Fort Reno served as one of the three remount depots that encompassed a time period of 1908 to 1947. Specialized horse breeding and training of mules became the central focus of activity. These horses and mules were shipped to other parts of the world during the two wars.

The fort had two museums, a fine chapel and many remaining buildings in generally good repair. The first museum had to do with the history of the fort and the other was a sort of cavalry museum. I was especially interested in the cavalry exploits during the Civil War and the Indian Wars and enjoyed the various mentions and pictures of General George Custer. One special horse garnered lots of attention in the Fort Reno museum. Black Jack, raised and trained here, was the riderless horse that was used in President John F. Kennedy's funeral procession as well as those of presidents

Hoover and Johnson and General McArthur.

German prisoners of war were kept on the post during World War II. These POWs built the existing chapel on the base.

My visit to Fort Reno was very enjoyable, although my mind couldn't forget the upcoming ride against the wind to exit the fort. I think that the wind blew harder at this time as I could barely make any headway against it. Relief finally came with a sharp left turn at the fort's outer gate, which then put the wind back on my right side.

Back on a much-improved pavement on Route 66, I rode ten miles to Yukon, the home of singing superstar Garth Brooks and actor Dale Robertson. Yukon was a neat little town of about 23,000 with lots of Route 66 signs and a couple of motels. It has plenty of modern businesses mixed with those that have Route 66 significance. Yukon was also the place where Route 66 crossed the Chisholm Trail, on which countless cows were sent to market in Abilene, Texas.

A more upscale area was ahead with the towns of Bethany and then Warr Acres. Lake Overholser was huge, and the wind was whipping up ocean-like waves as I passed by. By now, the temperature was 101, and the winds topped out at 45 mph as I completed 70 miles for the day just on the edge of Oklahoma City, where I would spend the night.

By this time on the Route 66 adventure, I was getting about 15-20 emails per day from interesting people around the country who suggested attractions, restaurants and even motels. This sharing of the ride with the readers continued as such a boost and enhancement to me as the days passed by. I missed the Washita National Battlefield Park, one of General Custer's historical sites, simply because I didn't want to take the time to ride there, visit and return to the route. Remember that ten minutes by car is probably close to an hour each way by bike. The suggestion sent to me was very much appreciated, and although I couldn't go that day, I have promised to return at a later date by vehicle and visit that site and more on my long list of "places still to see."

Now on to see the rest of Oklahoma.

CHAPTER (8)

t has been said that Route 66 put Oklahoma on the map, and it is often forgotten that the former territory had only reached statehood two decades before the establishment of the inter-state highway system in the 1920s. It was no fluke that the Mother Road was charted through Oklahoma. The state had suffered economically because many thought of it as Indian Territory, and Route 66 offered travelers a chance to see that Oklahoma was ready to join the 20th century.

This wonderful adventure was flying by, as evidenced by the fact that I was already riding on the 22nd day since starting in California. This was the first day with real rain. Clouds threatened, but only drizzled, back near Seligman, Arizona. Oddly enough to most people, I have no problems riding in the rain. Just a good brim on a hat and a thin rain jacket if needed have been enough protection. But after having experienced so much heat to this point, I didn't get the rain jacket out of my bag.

The biggest benefit of the unsettled weather as I rode into Oklahoma City was that the wind had finally settled down. It was cooler, and the lightning popped just close enough to keep me pedaling quickly. Though not really cool with a temperature in the upper 70s, I was glad for the pleasant break from the 90s and 100s.

An overnight at the Hospitality Inn had once again been restful, with breakfast for dinner from McDonald's. One disappointment was that I ordered ice cream that somehow didn't make it into the bag. Ice cream of some kind had again become a staple for nearly every day, almost all of them with the relentless heat. Although not much of an ice cream eater at home, my refreshment needs changed during those challenging days on the bike.

Oklahoma City was an oil boom town, with oil discovered here in 1928. At one time, 24 actual oil wells were pumping on the grounds of the state capitol.

Riding across Oklahoma City during morning rush hour was also a big challenge, but I had a good route, or so I thought. My map called for leaving Route 66 several times, but not in the way that I did it. Somehow, I got on a very fast expressway by mistake and was lucky to find my way off of it. But before I did get off, I pedaled on a slim shoulder in the dark. Vehicles flew by me, and I knew that they had a hard time seeing me, especially when I crossed the entrance and exit ramps. On a bright day with lesser traffic, I would have been worried about doing this, but this situation was truly scary. This was one of the scarier moments of my ride to this point and it became the unofficial start to my "good route." It was still dark when I exited the expressway. I actually found the right road but proceeded to get lost again in a neighborhood, then found myself on Route 66 again and headed east.

I passed the massive 45th Infantry Museum, the ASA Softball Museum, and a Firefighters Museum, all before 8 a.m. A huge thunderstorm, the one described on TV, had been building off to the west and was getting closer. I climbed a long hill with a small Route 66 park opposite some great tile work honoring the roadway and then passed a few souvenir shops. Suddenly, I was lost again but still headed east under threatening skies.

Convinced that I was on the wrong road, I stopped to study my map, and a motorist pulled over to help me. After I showed him where I needed to go, he gave me his thoughts on how to get back on 66. Two more guys taking a smoke break told me another way, but admittedly were not sure. Finally, with the rain about to hit, I stopped at a convenience store with a very helpful clerk. She seemed so confident when I asked the best way to reconnect and then named the roads I would cross if I continued straight ahead. Basically, all I had to do was keep riding east and the two roads would intersect, or so she said.

So I pedaled on and eventually found one of the roads that she mentioned, although I was then ten miles from where I wanted to be. Two local farmers explained just how to get back to Route 66 and that they were disappointed the convenience store beside us didn't have any breakfast biscuits on this morning. Of course, I was too.

By getting lost, I climbed more hills than I should have but still enjoyed the ride through beautiful farmland in the rain. I finally joined Route 66 near Luther after totally missing Arcadia. My one regret is that I missed the historic round barn there but added it to my list for things to see on the return trip.

Luther was a very small town of 1,200 residents, but I was surprised that it does have a Sonic that was very busy on this morning. More interesting to me was that Luther had the historical marker that signified the starting line of the Oklahoma Land Rush in 1889. After removing the Indians from the area, the U.S. government opened the land for settlement and over two million acres were claimed after noon on the first day.

Next came Wellston, unusual in that a Route 66B followed its own course through the business district. A pretty little downtown area that called itself the Pecan Capital of the World teemed with vehicles parked along the rainy Main Street, but I continued on back to Route 66 itself where a bustling truck stop was also the center of lots of traffic. Interstate 44 was nearby, and so many people in a hurry probably had something to do with my only close call of the whole journey.

Once away from the truck stop, I pedaled east on Route 66 and quickly came to a four-way stop with moderate traffic on each side. My experiences with four-way stops in the past had been pretty good, but I always made sure to look in the other directions twice each. In this case, this practice probably saved me from serious injury. When it came time to ride across the road and continue my journey, I realized that a truck was coming at high speed from the north. I waited, and watched him barrel through the intersection without slowing. There was nothing that I or the other drivers could do but watch him and wonder what might have just happened had I ridden into the intersection as soon as I had the right of way.

Pedaling ahead in the light rain with accompanying lightning and thunder took me into Chandler, the best of the towns during this day. Small bursts of heavy rain came, one of them just as I rode through the downtown area. Impressive were four of the older gas stations recycled into other businesses. Another one, the oldest Phillips station in town, had been renovated just enough to see the possibilities of future use.

Ahead was the Lincoln Motel, one of the oldest and most unique motels I had seen. Built in 1939, a series of duplex bungalows looked very inviting and well-kept. Had it been later in the day, I would certainly have explored the possibility of spending the night there. The last of the heavy rain began to dissipate as I left Chandler, reputed to be the site of the last old west gunfight in 1924.

Just down the road was Davenport, with at least two more of the renovated old gas stations. A popular use for the larger stations seemed to be cafes or coffee houses. I wondered often about the history of these old stations and what stories they might have told if that was possible. Quite often, I just pulled over and looked inside, especially interested in the bathrooms and work areas.

About nine miles later, I arrived in Stroud, my planned stopover for the night. The Skyliner Motel, built in 1939, was marketed as having one of the best neon signs on Route 66. I was glad to be here after 71 challenging miles for the day.

Route 66 had finally become its own road, with towns not dominated by the interstate. There were no shoulders most of the time, but the moderate traffic coexisted just fine with my bike. After riding through so many towns on the main thoroughfares, I had a sense of what the traveler of the 1940s and '50s might have experienced along the way. My friend the train had just about disappeared over the last few days even though the tracks were still visible. Those trains had been a constant in California, Arizona and New Mexico, something I found comforting because their own journey was similar to mine. I had not seen a moving train in two days.

As expected, Route 66 had now taken a slight northerly direction, moving away from the earlier easterly path. The wind had lessened significantly, and so had the extreme temperature, at least for the time being. Now, just a few days from Kansas and Missouri, I anticipated less extreme weather.

My stay in Stroud was a little disappointing, especially after the motel owner told me how busy the motel would be due to an Indian festival held locally. The room was by far the smallest I had seen, something the owner said was common for the construction date of the motel. He probably didn't realize that I had some experience with others of the time period and knew that larger ones were just as likely.

I did have space, just barely, to get my bike in the room. The bathroom and shower were tiny and some of the fixtures in the room appeared to be authentic to the 1939 period. I saw that the checkout notice appeared to be the original which made me wonder about the thousands of others who had overnighted in the room and read the same statement that I did. Regardless, the draw of the place was the huge sign that would come on just before dark. A bike ride to the other end of town took me to the Rock Café, built of the stone excavated when Route 66 was constructed over 70 years ago. It was now a popular local eatery that was recently restored after a serious fire. Who knew that Stroud was the home of the International Brick and Rolling Pin Festival?

Rain showers came in the evening as I waited for the sign to come on. Once it did, along with a few others staying in the motel, I went out to get some photos. As was the case with many of the bigger signs, this one had a section not working. Still, it was somewhat impressive, but not enough for the only real drawing card for the motel. I saw no evidence that anything had happened with the expected Sac and Fox Indian Festival, even with the huge banner across the street.

There is a park in Stroud where Indian athlete Jim Thorpe has been remembered. Thorpe, dubbed by many as the greatest athlete of the first half of the 20th century, played professional baseball and football and also won the decathlon and pentathlon gold medals at the Olympics. Part Sac and Fox Indian, Thorpe got his early education in Stroud.

The bed in my motel room was great, but with the room being so small, the AC unit was hard to adjust. I awoke several times during the night feeling very cold and eventually turned it completely off. In retrospect, I chose the Skyliner Motel because of a gimmick and promised myself to consider other choices the next time. There was another motel just around the corner that might have been the better accommodation.

My ride east out of Stroud was uneventful the next morning under cloudy skies. I rode with little traffic to Depew, where I planned a stop for a couple of egg and cheese biscuits. The convenience store closest to town was on Route 66, but sat alone away from the downtown area. After the egg biscuit stop, I saw the sign and pedaled toward the actual downtown although nobody else seemed headed that way. What I found was a mostly boarded-up Main Street, but one that obviously had some history. While I walked around taking some pictures, I noticed that Fred Jackson was watching me from his pickup truck. Fred pulled over to talk and proceeded to tell me about Depew from a lifelong resident's point of view. He told me that Depew was thriving in the 1950s with a movie theater, three groceries and all kinds of other stores in the downtown. When the oil boom played out, nearly all those stores closed up, leaving the deserted town that we saw on this morning. Fred told me to be careful on the road ahead as there were no shoulders and some heavier traffic when I approached Bristow.

Riding into Bristow turned out easier than expected, and I was surprised to see so many breakfast places with plenty of business. At one time, more millionaires lived here than in any other town in Oklahoma. Then it was on to Kellyville and another snack stop for me. Nice people, but I didn't linger.

Just after Kellyville, I met the first cyclist that I had seen going west on Route 66. Roy Leinfuss of Salida, Colorado, rode his long-distance bike and pulled a fully loaded trailer. Roy had already lost his camera and part of the usage of his phone to water damage but was optimistic about the rest of his trip. As usual, when two long-distance cyclists meet on the road, we shared quite a bit of recent information before we wished each other "Safe travels!" and pedaled away. This was my first Route 66 encounter with a solo rider who was out for multiple weeks at a time. Roy scheduled this trip a while back and said that he had already planned another for next summer. After thinking about his statement, it seems that mine was scheduled, as well. More on that later.

Sapulpa was the next town, about 20,000 strong, and was another community with a four-lane Route 66 main drag. A huge wall map of Route 66 on the outside of a bar showed how far I had progressed. Based on the map, I had almost completed two-thirds of the total distance of the most recent alignment.

The towns had started to come regularly, so I had stopped carrying my emergency water. Saving a few pounds helped a lot when climbing, and I had my eye on those upcoming Ozark Hills. Most of the remaining afternoon would be in Tulsa with lots of stores and plenty of chances to reload.

An older version of Route 66 briefly steered me away from the heavy traffic that headed into Tulsa, and in the words of Roy Leinfuss, "Through the hood!" Actually what happened was that a little-used section of 66 approached Tulsa through a low-end residential area and then morphed into more of an industrial zone. Then, suddenly, Route 66 was showcased on signs and a few elaborate displays including a water tower and train, and I found myself nearing the downtown area. Tulsa appeared to be very proud of its association with Route 66 and of its own beautiful streets. The downtown area was clean and attractive.

I stopped at Ollie's Restaurant, which proudly displayed its association with Route 66, for another piece of famous pie. Jack Connery, a Salisbury resident who had grown up in Tulsa, asked me to make sure of this stop. I told the manager my story and ordered a piece of peanut butter pie, to which he replied, "You know, that pie just doesn't look quite right to me. I am going to give you the rest of it and just charge for a slice." Of course, I agreed and saved the amazing pie for much later, once my ride was complete for the day.

The ride into town took a right as I pedaled past a fantastic mix of old and new architecture while the actual street numbers changed a couple of times, but still I could tell that Route 66 had been the foundation of this road for a long time. On my map, the ride out of town looked like it would take a while, and that turned out to be an understatement. Up and down little hills, often passing Route 66-era motels and through what seemed to be a hundred stoplights, I rode east as the day got hotter. I could tell on my map that 193rd Street appeared to be the last one before Tulsa would release me, and eventually it took 12 miles to make it to that turn-off. There were several construction projects in the works and a few tight places with barrels along the way. I enjoyed my visit to Tulsa, even though it seemed to take the whole afternoon.

Just about three miles from the long-in-coming end to Tulsa was Catoosa, another story in itself. Catoosa was famous for two things: gambling and the Blue Whale. Jack had told me not to miss the Blue Whale, and all my literature touted the whale as possibly the premier attraction of the whole "Mother Road." I knew it had to be good, and I didn't want to miss it.

By this time, finally with all the stoplights behind me, I was down to pedaling on fumes. Some type of boost was in order, and I needed to ask directions, so Wendy's seemed to be a perfect stop. I ordered a vanilla Frosty and a large Diet Coke, which, when taken together, had proven before to revive my legs on a hot day. While waiting, I asked the girl at the counter to tell me how to get to the Blue Whale. Her reaction was priceless, because her totally unin-terested reply went something like this: "I know it is around here somewhere, but I don't know where." The second Wendy's girl di-rected me to a third, the first of the trio over 30 years of age. She told me where to find it and that people asked the same question often and received much the same reply from the other girls. I began to think the Blue Whale may not be all I hoped for if these women didn't know where it was.

I finished my Frosty and drink and rode away, following the directions given. I took a right and then a left and found myself back on Route 66, which I didn't realize had turned previously. There on the left was the Blue Whale, a huge concrete structure of over 50 feet long that was originally built by Hugh Davis in 1972. Tourists walked into it and slid out one of its fins into the adjacent pond. It was my most cherished picture to date of Route 66 attractions. The people of Catoosa and the local Hampton Inn restored the Blue Whale to its original appearance with a fundraising effort that proved immensely popular.

Claremore was the next town, about 12 miles from Catoosa. The ride was on a very good portion of Route 66, made even more enjoyable after spending quality time with the Blue Whale. I did pass through a wreck that happened just ahead of me but everyone seemed to be fine. During this ride, I saw several trains on the tracks beside the road. Where had they been? Train sightings continued through my time in Claremore.

Will Rogers, born in Claremore, was Oklahoma's favorite son. Not a day had gone by since I entered Oklahoma that I had not seen or heard his name at some point. Rogers was a cowboy, actor, politician and so much more. Rogers made more than 70 movies as the public found his folksy Oklahoma twang and his clever way with words irresistible. He became one of the most popular radio personalities in the medium's earliest years. Rogers was also a proponent of aviation and an accomplished pilot who sadly lost his life in an airplane crash.

I stopped first at the Will Rogers Inn on Will Rogers Boulevard and inquired about the rate for a Will Rogers room for the night. It was high, as I expected it to be. I asked about other places, usually a pretty good tactic to get the price down some. It worked, but not enough, and I went outside and called the Claremore Inn, recommended by Adventure Cycling, which was not always a good thing. A good price, much better than the manager's special price at the Will Rogers Inn, sealed the deal. I headed to the Claremore and found one of the nicest and most hospitable desk clerks expecting me with a smile. Very professional and courteous, he checked me into a fantastic room, too. Once again, I made the right motel move and found myself about three to four miles farther along on Route 66 by the end of the day. Also, this motel with everything working and at a good price somewhat offset the experience at the Skyliner Inn in Stroud the night before.

A rather humorous situation played out when I had to go find something to eat. A Sinclair convenience store was next door and had a sign out for pizza. I walked over and found no pizza and none being prepared. I asked why the store had the sign, and he told me that I could instead get a good deal on a breakfast croissant. A language barrier hampered our discussion, but I almost had to escape the store because he kept offering me options for food that were of no interest to me. On down the street was a great convenience store with a bunch of late day "two for one" deals on pastries. Pretty soon, I was set for the evening. Once back in the room, I had a great planning session and was excited about another early start the next morning.

After staying up too late to watch the Olympic trials and the end of the NASCAR race, I experienced a little trouble dragging out of bed in such a nice room. Although harder to get out of bed than usual, once moving the pace picked up and I soon was on the road. Several times over the last ten days or so, I had thoughts of how wonderful that day's ride had been and how it stacked up in my list of all-time favorites. Little did I know that another of those days was evolving.

On this Sunday morning, I had the wide four-lane Route 66 all to myself as I left Claremore. As I had mentioned before, Sundays were almost always good, and I was excited to see what happened on this one. The morning warmed quickly, with not much of a breeze in any direction. I pedaled to a convenience store in Foyil, a very small town with at least one claim to fame. I bought a couple of egg and cheese biscuits and asked the clerks if there was anything interesting to see. They knew of nothing close by, but another customer mentioned the statue of Andy Payne and a small park on Andy Payne Boulevard. I knew of the legendary Payne and hoped to find the statue, but she told me where to see it and off I went.

Payne was a 20-year-old runner from Foyil who showed talent in high school races and then struggled after graduation to find a job. He moved to California and saw a flier for the first Transcontinental Foot Race. Payne raised the money to enter the race and won, running faster than older and more experienced runners from around the world. Payne's first-place prize was $25,000, an incredible sum in 1928. He paid off the family farm, bought land of his own and married his high school teacher. Payne never ran again, except for political office, and died a wealthy and revered man.

The next listed town was Bushyhead, but I never saw it. The action picked up when I pedaled into Chelsea, a town of about 2,000 residents. I thought later that it was common that some towns with 2,000 people seem to have little going on, especially on a Sunday morning. Not so with Chelsea. I already knew that the town had at least one unusual home that I wanted to see called the Hogue house. The materials for the house were purchased and delivered by railcar in 1913 for $16 from Sears and Roebuck. I knew that the house was still standing, and I tried to find it on the way into town. Looking for a small house, I had no success even though I had an address. So I headed farther into town to ask.

A quick stop at the convenience store turned out to be one of the nicest moments of my whole ride. I was inside for a few minutes getting some snacks, and when I came out, two nice-looking women waved at me to come over to their van. Stephanie and Danielle Wolf asked about my ride and where I was going today. After filling them in on my plans, they invited me to their church for breakfast. While I considered it, there was pedaling to do and many more miles to cover that day. I really enjoyed them and thought as I left just how nice it had been for them to wait on me and offer breakfast.

After some clarification from Stephanie and Danielle, I was able to find the Hogue house, Amazingly, I found a beautiful, two-story house that was still in use. I also found a prosperous little downtown and learned that Chelsea was famous for having the first oil well in Oklahoma, sinking the first successful well in 1889. With Route 66 running right through the center of the town, Chelsea was at least the second town that had an underground passageway to the other side of the very busy road. On my way out of town, I spotted a beautiful old bridge that was the last of its kind in Oklahoma. Will Rogers' sister lived here, and he is said to have visited here frequently.

The next town was White Oak, and just down the road was Vinita. I asked about and considered taking a six-mile side trip to visit a McDonald's that spans Interstate 44. I didn't go there after reminding myself that I would be backtracking and decided to keep going forward. It would have been interesting to see the fast-moving traffic passing by underneath my feet, but there was lots more to see ahead. TV's Doctor Phil hails from Vinita, but he didn't come out and wave.

Afton came next with a big truck stop and supposedly a big field of buffalo, but I didn't see any. On then to Miami as the afternoon heated up. I stopped at a convenience store for a drink and stood in a long line until waited on. All I wanted was the drink, and the clerk told me that I had to buy $5 of goods to use a debit card. I told her, "Maybe you should post that somewhere." She said, "Oh, it is!" and then moved a display out of the way of the sign. I told her, "Gosh, can't believe I missed it." Since this was a Sunday afternoon, street crews had chosen to pave Main Street through the downtown area while less traffic was about. I rode through town long enough to see the Coleman Theatre that opened in April, 1929, just six months before the start of the Great Depression. Early performers included Tom Mix, Will Rogers, Sally Rand and the Three Stooges.

Since Main Street was also Route 66, I rode past the paving and pedaled out of town. A short segment that was later abandoned in the area was unusual in its own right. When money was short for the paving of a certain distance, instead of just paving half the length of the road, the crews chose to pave the whole length but only one lane wide. Later, when cars met each other, both would drop one side of the car off the pavement and keep going. This idea didn't work for long.

Another little town had been on my mind all day, actually for several days after I realized that it was on Route 66. Commerce, Oklahoma, was the childhood home of Mickey Mantle, my biggest boyhood hero. I have followed the New York Yankees, Mantle's professional baseball team, since I was a small boy. Not sure exactly how I heard of Mantle and his exploits to begin with, but I remembered checking his stats back in the day when the newspapers still printed the major league box scores daily. The Yankees' place in the standings was the second thing I checked. By the time I entered Commerce, Mantle's home and a statue of him as a Yankee at his high school were two must-sees. I didn't have a detailed map of

Commerce, so I stopped at the first open business in town to get some help.

Just across the street from that stop, I noticed with interest a 1929 Conoco service station that advertised the ability to work on flying saucers, marking the first time I have heard such a unique statement. Next, I talked with the owner of the consignment store, who was a resident of Commerce. She said that her husband was a big Mantle fan, too, but she didn't know much except that the statue was at the baseball field. She didn't know where the family house was, but she had heard that a resident wanted to make it a museum. I left the shop and headed down the street and immediately spotted the turn for Mantle's home on South Quincy Street and didn't make any effort to contain my excitement.

Never having seen Mantle play in person, I did see him when he visited Salisbury. Pedaling down the street, I noticed quickly that it was only a few blocks long. Then I saw the house, and it was almost surreal that I was in the yard of the man who had been one of the greatest baseball players ever. No one else was around. The modest white house had a plaque on the front recognizing Mantle's childhood and his later baseball prowess. Period furniture was still inside, and I wondered if it was the same furniture that Mantle used as a kid. I was able to see virtually throughout the house from the doors and windows.

One of the interesting stories told in one of my guidebooks was that when hitting the baseball in the yard, Mantle was instructed to hit the tin storage building with the ball. A hit in a certain place was ruled a double, another place was a triple and yet another place was good for homer. Mantle's dad and granddad played baseball with him almost every day.

I left and rode just a short distance away to the high school and quickly spotted the baseball field. A man worked on preparing the field for a game, and I thought about asking him to take my picture there but he never looked up as I went by. Just past the outfield wall was the statue that captured Mantle on his follow through after swinging at a pitch while with the Yankees.

The visit to Commerce was an incredible highlight for me. I grew up in a similar house but with all the room I needed to hit a baseball. This man with such incredible talent had lived here, right where I stood on this day. Nothing about this day would be forgotten.

On to Quapaw, and nobody seemed to notice. Late on this Sunday afternoon, the most interesting thing in town was a super large agricultural sprayer that moved into a field just ahead of me to begin his work. Watching huge farm equipment operate had always been one of my favorite pastimes, another interest that was spawned as a small child.

And finally for the evening after 86 miles, I ended the day in Baxter Springs, Kansas. The state line came just before the town limits, beginning a very short visit to Kansas. It's my second visit overall, the first coming during my cross-country ride of 2013. I had a great deal at another wonderful motel called the Baxter Inn, just beside a Casey's General Store on one side and a McDonald's on the other. Ice cream and plenty of food sealed off the memory of yet another fantastic day. This day's experience would be hard to top for the rest of the journey but there was plenty more riding to do.

One early concern about this trip was that my route took in a good portion of Tornado Alley. Some of my guidebook and map information pointed out that Quapaw and Baxter Springs both suffered extensive damage during four days of successive tornadoes in 2014. More than 80 tornadoes were confirmed during the outbreak that resulted in 36 fatalities and more than 300 injuries. Upwards of 150 homes and other structures were destroyed in the two towns.

Tornado Alley is particularly prone to supercell thunderstorms, the breeding ground for violent tornadoes. The "dryline," a front that separates the moist air from the Gulf of Mexico and the dry air of the Southwest, often remains over the region that includes north Texas, Oklahoma and Kansas along Route 66. But there was no place that I would rather be on this day and this cycling adventure!

CHAPTER (9)

Into Missouri and another round of the Ozark Hills

went to bed last night in Baxter Springs thinking that the out-look for today was not the best. High temperatures and winds were predicted to combine with my second journey into the Ozark hills, a venture that I had not looked forward to since first committing to the Route 66 ride. Based on the maps, choices for lodging and camping were limited ahead. Add to all that the fact that I turned off the TV too late and overslept for the second time. The delay was just about an hour, and I hated seeing the day-light already so bright as I still packed my bags. My internal alarm clock was usually all I needed to stay on time, but that function failed this time. Regardless, I was going to make the best of my poor start.

Grabbing a small amount of the limited continental breakfast at the wonderful Baxter Inn, I pushed the bike out the door. Right away, and somewhat odd for me, I decided to just take it easy and make sure that I didn't miss anything in order to make better time. On the few occasions that I had overslept on these rides, it usually felt right to push the pace to make up the time. I found right away that Baxter Springs was loaded with history, especially Civil War history, and I had to find out more before leaving town.

The "Baxter Massacre" battle site was particularly intriguing. Most of a Union detachment was wiped out by the Confederates on the edge of town in 1862, and many of them were buried locally.

A small park commemorated the battle.

Local legend has it that Jesse James robbed one bank in town and tried to rob another. I looked for the right buildings but couldn't find them. At one time, Baxter Springs was considered the toughest town in Kansas. The downtown area was very pleasant with a nice mix of older and newer buildings.

Known as "The First Cow Town in Kansas," Baxter Springs served as the northern terminus of a primary branch of the legendary Shawnee Trail. The trail was the first of several routes used pre- and post-Civil War to move stock north to the Midwest. Cattlemen would drive their herds from Texas to Baxter Springs, then lay over to fatten them up before they shipped or drove them to Kansas City, St. Joseph, Sedalia or St. Louis.

Another story on Mickey Mantle concluded like this: Mantle, from just across the state line in Oklahoma, played with the Baxter Springs Whiz Kids for several years. Mantle hit a home run into the Spring River and was approached by a scout from the New York Yankees after the game, and the rest became history. Mantle was enshrined along with other local baseball stars in a Little League Museum.

I rode into Riverton and then on to Galena. I did look around briefly in both towns, but for some reason, Route 66 was in such a poor state of repair that the riding was very rough. Kansas has only 12 miles on Route 66, and I found a claim that Kansas was the first to pave their portion of the "Mother Road." Oddly enough, on this morning it seemed that very little work had been done on these roads since. Galena had lots of murals on the sides of buildings and a wonderfully restored depot.

The next town was Joplin, Missouri. I had earlier visited here on my cross-country ride in 2013 and didn't remember struggling as much to get through the town. I got off the mapped route and stayed on the actual Route 66 and then tried to use my phone and maps to connect again after passing through the middle of town. Joplin doesn't believe in bike lanes, but they did believe in turning their street-side grates lengthwise. Certainly, this issue hadn't affected the tires on cars, but the tires of a bike would fall right through. To make matters even more challenging, not every grate was turned the same way. Now having ridden through thousands of towns, this was the very first time that any grates were installed this way. Only once did my front tire fall between the metal strips, and luckily there appeared to be no damage to the spokes as I pulled it back out and slowly continued on. Joplin is the hometown of actor Dennis Weaver, Chester of "Gunsmoke" fame.

I had promised myself to not worry about lost time, but concerning thoughts crept in as more delays occurred. The Ozark hills began, and Joplin had so many very long stoplights, long enough for an interested truck driver beside me to ask about my ride as I waited to turn left. With the help of a Joplin utility worker who was familiar with the surrounding area, I began to make up a little time and follow the route more easily. At least two versions of 66 were close by, but they were clearly labeled as the older and newer versions. I was on the newer one.

The next two towns were Webb City and Carterville. Webb City was a mining town after the discovery of lead nearby. The downtowns of both were pretty good with lots of historic homes, and I only was briefly lost once as I searched for the Route 66 Historic Missouri Byway signs.

On to Carthage, the biggest town since Joplin and home to the amazing Jasper County Courthouse. The courthouse sat on the top of a hill in the center of the downtown, easily seen from anywhere in the area. On the day that I rode through, there was lots of construction on the nearby streets, but I had to ride to the top of the hill just to get a closer look at this magnificent building.

Another unusual attraction was the 1939 Boots Court Motel that I didn't know anything about ahead of time. Each room had a little carport, and a sign said, "A Radio in Every Room!" TVs were not in the rooms. This was another example of the time of day not being right for choosing a motel. Otherwise, this one would have certainly been interesting for a night's lodging.

Carthage had also been the site of an 1861 Confederate Civil War victory, and Marlin Perkins of early "Wild Kingdom" fame was born here.

I stopped in a nice convenience store and loaded up with plenty of goodies for the road which later turned out to be great choice. My plan was to stay on Route 66 even though it was folly based on my map. I told the clerk what I had in mind and asked her about shoulders on the road, the reason that the bike map didn't want me to use it. She wasn't sure, but she thought that Route 66 did have shoulders on the road to Springfield. The maps were several years old, and I thought it was worth taking a chance to stay on the real road instead of detouring for a better road of less interest.

Route 66/Highway 96 left Carthage and headed toward Springfield, starting with good roads and a two-foot shoulder which was a boon for me that lasted ten miles. Suddenly, the dreaded rumble strips appeared on the road, leaving a cyclist very little room to ride. My pace began to slow, and my unmentioned goal of making Springfield to spend the night was slowly ebbing away. The Ozark hills had begun in earnest, too, a constant up and down with no real end in sight for many miles.

The pummeling sidewind was back as well, with rising temperatures, so I planned to resupply at one of the upcoming towns. Enthusiastically, I rode into Avilla and on through Phelps. Both looked big enough to have a store or two but did not. I just had to laugh and keep riding. The dots on the map looked much bigger than the crossroads that often have a thriving convenience store or two. My water was running low, and I considered stopping at a small business or house, but none looked promising. I pedaled on to a crossroads that I think was Albatross and found a small convenience store that saved the day. With my drinks and a few fresh snacks, I asked the clerk about any available motels between there and Springfield. With a very pleasant demeanor, she smiled and dug out a map to show me what she thought was the best option. While not sure of the exact road off Route 66, the clerk described a truck stop that had a family owned motel. She told me to ask again for the correct road to turn toward the interstate when I got closer.

Back on Route 66, I stopped at the post office in Halltown to get some further directions. I found the door to the desk locked but knew that a car was still there, parked in a way that suggested it belonged to someone who worked there. After returning to the bike and retrieving some of my warm water to drink, I saw the postmaster coming toward me with a bottle of cold water. She told me how to find the motel and that she personally recommended it because she knew the family that owned the whole truck stop.

I pedaled on over some long up-and-down hills while looking for the turnoff once I heard the trucks rumbling in the distance. That sound was usually comforting to me as I rode along, because having the interstate in the area meant at least some version of a safety valve should any kind of trouble occur. While climbing one more Ozark hill to ride into the truck stop, I didn't see the motel at first amid several large buildings. After asking in the 24-hour restaurant with breakfast all day, I was directed toward Hood's Motel, yet another wonderful choice with a small glitch.

Without ever before staying in a truck-stop motel, I had no idea what to expect. Most of the over-the-road tractor-trailers had their own living quarters, so I doubted there was much demand for the accommodations from the drivers. In fact, most of the vehicles parked outside the rooms when I arrived were work pickup trucks of some type. After 79 miles for the day, I had arrived a little later in the afternoon than I had hoped for. I asked at the desk about a non-smoking single room for one night and was told that only a few rooms remained. My concerns were to make sure of the WiFi, and of course the price needed to be reasonable. The owner, working the desk when I came in, took care of me on both and I quickly had the bike and myself in the room.

The quality of the room was surprising indeed. Most of the places that I found with good pricing for single-night rooms were very basic, but this was not the case at Hood's. This room was nice, with every single item of good quality, and wonderfully clean. A favorite thing for me was the Bible in the room, already open and turned to a chosen page for the day. Even the ice machine for the motel was in a nicely decorated area with live plants, something I hadn't seen before.

Now for the glitch. I noticed upon entering the room that there were a few flies already inside, or maybe they had followed me in. I had experienced something similar quite often, especially since the air temperature was so hot. A game that I played fairly well was to knock out any flies in the room before I could relax totally. It took a while this time, breaking my thought pattern often as I prepared my newspaper submission. Confident that I had them all, it was easy to complete my work and think about a trip to the restaurant for a huge, late-afternoon breakfast.

Down to the restaurant I went and ordered that breakfast and then up the hill again to the convenience store for some ice cream and waters. With all that done, on the way back to the motel, I was asked by the owner if everything in the room was as expected.

He said, "If you have any trouble with the TV remote, just let me know." I hadn't tried the TV but did as soon as I went in the room, and I couldn't get it to work. Going back out to where the owner and his wife sat, I asked him to come show me the trick to make it work. He did, and I realized that this was a hi-tech system that was much more directional than usual. But just before leaving, he said, "Sorry about the flies. We had two livestock trucks here last night and I believe they left all their flies with us."

Back to the room and ravenously hungry, my new crop of flies required my immediate attention. After ten minutes, I had them all and vowed not to open the door again until I was leaving the next morning. The food and ice cream hit the spot and I settled in for another night of good rest ahead of riding into Springfield and then on to more of the seemingly never-ending Ozark hills. By now, I knew that I loved the Missouri people but despised their hills and rumble strips.

The weather forecast was daunting for the day as I prepared the next morning to ride toward Springfield, about 15 miles away. The meteorologist on TV called for storms to start about 8 a.m., but the sky didn't look particularly threatening as I rode away from Hood's Motel. It was hard to say goodbye to the nice truck-stop motel that some wonderful people helped me find.

Springfield was also a part of my 2013 cross-country ride, but not because it was on the Adventure Cycling map. I remember being frustrated with the mapped route and asked about another option to my planned overnight stop. At the time, I didn't know if it was OK to ride a bike on the interstate in Missouri and asked several Springfield residents and got some comical answers. One customer at a convenience store told me that he had seen others do it and never noticed anyone being stopped. His advice was, "If I was you, I would do it and claim ignorance if stopped. You won't get a ticket." I jumped on the interstate that afternoon and made good headway to close out a long day in the rain.

Speaking of rain, as I got closer to Springfield during rush hour, the clouds began to close in from the northwest. Traffic kept building until I passed an expressway and Interstate 44, then calmed down as I neared the downtown. Springfield had a beautiful and largely walkable downtown area. Bass Pro Shops was headquartered there and has hosted a "Typewriter Toss" each Secretary's Day during April. Contestants threw typewriters at a target from 30 feet away.

Just as I passed the center of downtown, the first raindrops fell. The sky still didn't look particularly threatening, and it was warm already. I didn't pull out my rain jacket because those first drops were cooling and felt great. As I headed out toward more of the Ozarks, the intensity of the wind and rain gradually increased enough that I rethought taking the rain jacket out and putting it on. The jacket never came out of the bag but should have. The next two hours were on the Adventure Cycling course, but I was sure that I had made a wrong turn as the heavy rain and wind pounded the bike. The temperature dropped enough during the storm that my body was cold all over, although it was too late now to retrieve the jacket.

This was one of those downpours that made each car and truck spray me with cold water as they passed by. Finally, several miles past where I thought the turn should be, I found that I had been on the right road all along. I rode into Strafford, just a small exit for I-44 with a convenience store. It was amazing that I could have been so warm for days and now found my hands and upper body very cold, even more so after I entered the convenience store that seemed frigid. Back outside, there was some relief as the wind and rain both had lessened now that the worst of the storm had passed by.

The next stop was Marshfield, another town that I met in 2013. Edwin Hubble, the creator of the famous space telescope, came from Marshfield. A long afternoon began to develop as I pedaled up and down through Conway and Phillipsburg, together totaling a population of about 1,000 residents. My Route 66 guidebook listed nothing in the two towns to see, but I did enjoy the cows, pastures, corn and everything farming along both sides of the road.

My goal for this day was Lebanon, a town that I had a personal business history with even though I had never visited it. Lebanon was one of the towns that resided in the fescue grass production area, important to the horticultural industry where I worked for many years. Once into town, I called and asked about another of the famous motels along Route 66, the Munger Moss Motel. Another fantastic neon sign was part of the draw, but so was the history of the place. Lucky enough to have been on Route 66 and still near the superslab of Interstate 44, the motel was listed as classy and historic at the same time. During my call, I found that the motel was on the other end of Lebanon, and the owner told me that there were no food sources close by.

I chose to stop at a grocery in the downtown area since my bags were just about empty. Not sure that I would have a microwave or refrigerator, I took a chance and bought a few things that would need them. My purchases probably weighed 15 pounds, partly because of the small watermelon since the store had no sliced pieces. Struggling slightly to find a way to get all of the purchases in my bike bag, I didn't notice a man walk up to me from behind. Mark introduced himself and asked about the intent of my ride and how far I had traveled. After a brief conversation that included some laughter, Mark asked me if we could pray together for my continued safety as I headed toward Chicago. The words of his prayer were very moving while our heads were bowed in the store lot. I will never forget the effort that Mark made and his touching words.

Next was the search for the childhood home of a friend from Salisbury. Dr. Karl Hales from Catawba College asked me to look for it and I found the address, but not the correct house, which was disappointing. Then it was on to the motel, just about the last thing in Lebanon on the east side of town.

I got my room and had an interesting talk with the owner, who described the history of the motel and showed me some photos from earlier years. After 75 grueling miles for the day, I was happy to be at the Munger Moss Motel but a little disappointed that there was not a room refrigerator or microwave and no ice machine, either. The room itself was nicely decorated in a way that made the 70-year-old room look very attractive. To make up for a few of the shortcomings, I walked back down and asked the owner if I could get some ice and if she could microwave a sandwich that I bought at the store. She readily agreed and told me something about the history of the sign and the current cost of the upkeep. A small portion of one side of the sign was not working, and I was advised to take my pictures from the good side. The owner predicted a cost of about $2,000 to get it working again because the same repair was done last year.

My plan for the evening was to soak up the history of the place and then settle in for the Major League Baseball All-Star Game on TV. Last year on this special evening, I was just across the Ohio River from Cincinnati while traveling the Underground Railroad and enjoyed an up-close encounter with the fighter jets that flew over the 2015 all-star opening ceremonies. This year, watching on TV from Lebanon, Missouri, was just fine with me.

After several trips out to see the neon sign and get some photos, I watched about seven innings of the All-Star Game and fell into a very sound sleep in a great bed. I never ate the small watermelon and left it in the room so that hopefully someone would get it later.

Feeling energetic, I faced possibly the worst of the Ozark climbing days and expected fewer miles and not as much in scenery. I left early with no great expectations for the day. The first four hours of riding was just a long series of very challenging ups and downs, done over and over again at a very slow average pace of just over six miles per hour.

Hazelgreen was just a little settlement with a big truck stop and a bridge that I was very interested in. I had seen a poster about saving the Gasconade River Bridge while at the Munger Moss Motel in Lebanon and knew that there was a detour around the bridge, but I didn't know anything else. My cycling map gave the only option as riding on Interstate 44 to bypass the bridge and a closed section over the river. I did it this way but caught a brief glimpse of the bridge to my right as I had to pedal quickly through a tight spot of bridge construction on the interstate, thinking what a beautiful bridge it was.

Not always the best rule follower, I thought of retracing my steps on the interstate by walking against traffic to get at least a better view and picture. I quickly realized that this wasn't safe, so I looked for a better way to see the bridge. The closed portion of Route 66 showed up just below the interstate, and a wide and damp weedy area was the buffer between the two. Since there was not a fence, I rolled the bike down the hill and picked the best way across the weedy area to access Route 66. Once there, I rode several hundred feet back toward the bridge and found the road blocked with something similar to braced up car bumpers. The river below was also gated off but had a slim area where I could walk through the fence. A quick walk down to the river over very rocky terrain gave me a great view from the river bed of the underneath of the bridge. Two fisherman floated by but didn't notice me.

I walked back up the steep hill and pushed the bike down to the bumper blockers and leaned it against them before walking out on the bridge. Already, I understood the desire by the local group to save the bridge. Huge and majestic, I envisioned the many cars heading to California and Chicago as they passed through this hilly and rural area of Missouri. Save the bridge!

After another serious climb on the interstate, I was able to access Route 66 again and ride into historic Waynesville. I was at the highest elevation for the town when I entered from the west and coasted for miles downhill while looking for two historic areas.

The first area was a park beside Roubidoux Creek where the Cherokee Indians from the Trail of Tears were forced to camp on their way to Oklahoma. Lots of historical markers gave information on the Indians and their suffering during the march to their new reservation. I walked around and read every marker while visualizing the Indians here on that long-ago day. The creek, larger than some rivers I had seen so far, passed under a five-span concrete arch bridge built in 1923, before Route 66.

Then, just a block or two away was a 140-year-old historical building that was used at various times for a hotel, Civil War hospital and a stagecoach stop. During the Civil War, Union troops built a fort to protect the telegraph lines between Springfield and St. Louis. Because the building was in a busy area of government activities, I struggled to find the best place for pictures and soon realized that the building was not open anyway. Waynesville was named after "Mad" Anthony Wayne, the Revolutionary War hero.

Waynesville had a lot of traffic for a small town, and it was hard for me to jump into it on the way out of town. Route 66 went up one of the steepest hills yet, on and on, reclaiming the drop in elevation from the west. On sort of a breakdown lane, I struggled to make the top. Along the way, I saw another well-known trademark of the town. A huge rock that the citizens thought looked like a frog has been painted that way and looked out over the cars climbing the hill.

The next town, hard to distinguish from Waynesville, was St. Robert. An unusual fact was that St. Robert was not established until 1951 and apparently had something to do with the U.S. Army's Fort Leonard Wood and the increased local population associated with it.

After finally reaching the top of the long hill that I hadn't expected, the riding was slightly easier. My curiosity was up about a place called "Devil's Elbow." The cycling map sent me onto an older version of Route 66 that was immediately bumpy and rough due to poor maintenance or no maintenance at all. The road through this area was narrow and curvy but did cross a much nicer one-lane bridge that ushered me toward a tree-blocked view of the Big Piney River. The road continued with another sharp turn or two across another bridge with a better view of the river before I headed back toward a more recent version of Route 66.

A sharp right turn onto a four-lane section of Route 66 through an almost deserted area was very odd, in my opinion. I struggled on yet another long hill to climb back out of the Devil's Elbow area. There was nothing impressive about this portion of the ride although I could understand why the section was later dropped as unsafe. The many tight curves and poor visibility probably played into the decision. During this time, the heat and humidity seemed highest for the day, and sweat dripped off my elbows continually, a sure sign that I was struggling to climb a long hill. On reaching the top of the Route 66 hill, I was directed right back onto the interstate where for the first time I noticed serious-looking storm clouds coming from the west.

Those clouds brought lightning and rain as I pedaled past the town of Doolittle, named after World War II flying hero Jimmy Doolittle. Doolittle led the bombing raid on Japan with B-25 Mitchell bombers flown off the carrier USS Hornet. By now, I knew that serious weather was coming and began to pedal as hard as I could for Rolla, the next larger town. A black sky brought sudden gale-force winds from my left side as the storms approached with rain so hard that I could barely see. Now in the only serious storm situation of the whole trip, I knew that I needed to reach cover as soon as possible. Rolla was still at least ten miles away by the time the storm had enveloped me with its full force.

Cars were slowing down due to heavy rain, but my only choice was to try and speed up even more. My Route 66 ball cap was blown off even though I had tightened it while securing my bags just before the heavy rain hit. Once again, I had not pulled out my raincoat and was not about to stop to get it now. With about five miles to go, I realized that my back tire was slowly going flat and quickly said a frantic prayer asking that the tire hold enough air to make it to Rolla. Beyond that, I just kept pedaling for all I was worth.

Finally, through the heavy rain, I noticed the sign for the Route 66 exit into Rolla and saw several motel signs, too. With just enough air in the tire to support the bike, I saw an Econo Lodge directly beside me on the interstate separated only by a downhill bank and the service road. Instead of continuing to the exit, I got off the bike and rolled it down the hill, across a ditch with a foot or so of rushing water, and right under the overhang of the Econo Lodge. By that time, whatever the price they asked was going to be fine with me as the rain and lightning followed me to their door.

Two nice ladies handed me a towel and then a very reasonable price, and within minutes, I rolled my bike into an especially big room. The desk ladies didn't know that I had a flat tire but they did know that I had a lot of drying out to do. I can't describe how nice it was to step inside that dry room where once again I had no immediate desire for air conditioning because of being soaked to the bone.

My clothes were dirty and nasty wet, and some of my other clothes needed attention, too, so I just threw all of them in a pile where they would wait until I got some detergent for a good washing. Once in dry clothes from my panniers, I walked to the Denny's next door and ordered a huge pancake and egg breakfast that would go a long way toward offsetting a very hard 62-mile day. Later, after the rain subsided enough to do it, I walked to a nearby convenience store and added to my water and snack supply. A small box of detergent for a dollar got the clothes washing and drying under way while I ate the huge amount of food.

The tire repair came next, but not before taking a few extra minutes to thank God for allowing that tire to hold enough air so that I could make it to shelter. I could hardly imagine how miserable it would have been to dig through my bags and repair that tire in the driving rain and wind. Time and again, those prayers have protected me. This was the third time during my trips that a tire repair occurred in the motel room. Not a bad place to be. The rain and lightning continued through most of the night, but I slept wonderfully yet again.

I forgot to mention that Rolla was actually named after Raleigh, N.C., but I never heard the reasoning for the unusual spelling. Early morning weather forecasts called for more storms and had plenty of pictures of the destruction from the previous evening. Many residents were left with trees down and the resulting loss of power. With my repaired tire, gone flat from more pieces of steel belting, and clean clothes, I rolled out the door into a cloudy morning.

I already knew that the local bike shop didn't open until 10 a.m.

so I hoped the tire was truly fixed. I found out that Rolla was also on the Cherokee Trail of Tears, as was a good portion of my route back toward Springfield. A surprising number of motels were at the same exit where I landed, but none as close as the Econo Lodge during my time of need. The famous Totem Pole Trading Company was right beside the Econo Lodge.

Riding east and now slightly north out of Rolla, I entered Northwye and pedaled out quickly by climbing a big hill into St. James. The noteworthy stop during this early morning sweep of local towns was the only vacuum cleaner museum I had ever seen. The Tacony Company in St. James provided the museum, posting that vacuum cleaners had been used as early as 1910. I didn't tour the museum, but others were.

On to Cuba, over some of the most reasonable terrain of the last few days. I found the world's largest rocking chair, 40 feet tall and certified by Guinness in 2008, outside a small general store along Route 66. Cuba was called "Mural City," and there were dozens of them painted on the sides of local buildings. Most depicted early residents or businesses.

Next came two pleasant little towns called Bourbon and Sullivan, both next to I-44. From there, I pedaled into Stanton, the home of the Meramec Caverns. The caverns, opened in 1935, were the subject of one of those great marketing campaigns using barn roofs and countless billboards. Since the caverns were just a few miles off of Route 66, I considered riding that way but added them to my list to see later. The caverns were reported to have been a Jesse James hideout, another tourism draw for the area.

The Jesse James Wax Museum was on Route 66, unusual in that the staff tries to convince those who enter that James didn't die of a gunshot in 1881 but lived until 1952. I did talk to a foreign couple on a motorcycle who had just toured the museum but were not convinced. They decided to spend the afternoon at the caverns.

An interesting segment of my trip began as I pedaled through St. Clair with nothing noteworthy to be seen. My cycling map called for a huge climb after crossing the Bourbeuse River, and the claim was not an exaggeration. This was the hardest climb of a day that was not as challenging overall as the previous day, either for weather or number of serious hills. This climb did top out at the highest point for the day and included a few nice views that were not common in the Ozarks because there is usually so much up and down that long-distance views just don't happen.

My cycling map and guidebook both recommended lodging for the night called the Gardenway Motel. It was a "must stay" per the guide book, but I could not get an answer at the motel after repeated calls. The phone did ring, and I left a message multiple times. An employee at a store in Stanton assured me that the motel was open and made sure I knew how to find it. With that assurance, I felt good about the motel even with no one answering the phone. This had certainly happened before and things had been fine later.

Just a few miles earlier, I had passed the Sunset Motel which was reputed to be closed but was obviously open. Sure enough, just a few miles farther on was the obviously closed Gardenway Motel. It still looked pretty good, so I expect the closing had been a recent decision. With my night's plans now up in the air, I continued on. The Travelodge was already exceptionally high and charged extra, $10 each, for a refrigerator and microwave. It was the only place around and any food would have to come from a small convenience store. There was no reason to delay, so I pedaled downhill into Pacific where my maps listed three of the higher priced chain motels.

Pacific had some extended cliffs along the left side of the road with lots of holes in them that were caused when silica was mined there. Those holes were perfect move-ins for a cliff dweller in my opinion. A chance conversation with a convenience store employee in Pacific provided the information that more reasonable motels were just ahead in Exeter. I followed his advice and seven more miles of easy pedaling helped me find an affordable America's Best Value Inn with another big plus, a Denny's right next door. I was right down the street from Six Flags Over Mid-America, the gigantic theme park.

Another large breakfast for dinner filled the bill for my evening and helped replace the calories of 86 more Ozark miles. Those nice folks at Denny's gave me plenty of extra water, and I was set for the evening as more thunder rumbled in the distance. Good thing, because no other stores were close by. I was ready to head for St. Louis and then on to Illinois. I certainly wanted to see the Gateway Arch and visit again with my old friend, the mighty Mississippi River.

CHAPTER ⑩

Across the Mississippi and the Illinois experience

Crossing the Mississippi River was just a day away, signaling a sort of exodus from the areas of westward expansion into the older and more established portion of America. But first, there were several stops that I wanted to make in St. Louis. I was near the end of the Ozarks and was glad to leave behind the very challenging road through about 50,000 square miles of relentless hills.

I woke with just about 35 miles remaining before reaching St. Louis. It looked as if my entry into the city would be around midday, probably a good time because the roads would be fairly well-traveled during the morning hours. The first roads would also be quite challenging, especially if I stayed on the route provided by the cycling map. A quick stop at a convenience store added a few things to my bags, but it wouldn't be long until I was in a city environment with plenty of supply available.

The first serious climb was through a residential area over a road closed for gas line work. I just kept riding past the workers and nobody said anything to me, especially good because I had no idea how to get around this road otherwise and join back with Route 66. A portion of it was so steep going up that I had to push the bike, but I finally reached the top of the climb and then rode downhill until I found what should have been Route 66, even though there were no signs. Then came another long and serious climb that finally topped out before I was completely spent. One interesting part of that ride was a work van that had problems was climbing the same road and not going much faster than me. A narrow breakdown lane was not wide enough for us both, so it was good to see that he could continue on, although much of the long line of traffic behind him probably preferred that he pull over.

Ellisville was the first town, at a time that I was convinced my early ride had nothing to do with Route 66. But as soon as I hit the town, the Route 66 signs for Missouri were back in play and would be all the way to St. Louis. Very flashy and new looking, Ellisville didn't match most of the older towns through which I had ridden for nearly a month. Traffic was moderate, with lots of bike lanes and those smooth, new concrete sidewalks along the way.

Now, with a direct shot into St. Louis on the same road, I just pedaled ahead and joined with the steadily increasing traffic but still often with a bike lane. The long road was now called State Road 100, and it went through several suburb towns including Ballwin, Manchester, Des Peres, Brentwood and Maplewood. What happened next started a sequence of very unusual happenings within about an hour. I had just ridden across an intersection and looked down to spot a very nice wallet with a few dollars underneath it. I hopped off the bike and walked back to pick it up and then got out of traffic to check the contents.

The wallet contained several credit cards and other things, too, but only $3 in cash. The owner of the wallet was from Connecticut. I put the wallet in my bag and pondered what to do with it. At the time, I wasn't sure exactly which of the towns I was in and didn't want to stop to find a police station. Sure that I would be in St. Louis within just a few minutes, I put it out of mind and concentrated on traffic and looking for a bike shop in the endless strip malls on both sides of the street. Not five minutes later, I spotted a guy walking toward a bike shop on the left and watched as he put a key in the door. This was perfect timing to pick up a few supplies and ask a couple of questions.

After pulling off to the edge of my lane, I waited for traffic to clear on both sides of the road and pushed the bike across the street quickly to head for the bike shop. While the owner turned on the lights, I told him that I needed two CO_2 cartridges and a replacement tube since I used the one in Rolla. While I paid for these, I asked about going to the Gateway Arch in St. Louis. The bike shop owner said I could see it for miles and asked if I had any other questions. My concern was what to do with the bike and all my bags and other gear during the time of my tour. Last night, I had emailed the ticket information office for the arch and was told by an email reply that there was no place to put the bike inside or any other protected area. The message said, "Just lock it up," to which I replied that the bike was a touring and endurance style with my clothes, supplies and tools in bags that couldn't be locked. I got no further reply. The bike shop owner understood and suggested asking at one of the big hotels in the area. His great idea was food for thought and exactly what I planned to do.

Back on the bike and pedaling east after a very productive early morning, I pulled into a St. Louis QT convenience store, one of the nicest ones that have everything. It was warm already and I needed a boost, so I bought a few things including a big pastry. Just as I came back out of the store, I noticed a guy who hopped out of his car very quickly and ran into the store. As soon as he entered the building, his car started rolling backwards toward the gas pumps. Once it started rolling, I took off running and opened the door, jumped into the seat and hit the brakes, then set the parking brake. Now with the car stopped for sure in the middle of the lot, I got back out of the car and went in search of the driver. Without finding him, I came back out just as he started to drive away. I yelled and he stopped, then realized that he had no idea what had happened and why his car was in the lot instead of the parking place where he left it. I told him that it was me who had stopped the car and he immediately seemed quite embarrassed. We talked a little longer and he gave me some good directions before we parted with kind words for each other, closing out that little adventure.

Back on the bike, I headed for the waterfront of St. Louis and my first sight of the Gateway Arch. Just a few minutes later I saw it and continued until the same street ended in a dead end just south of the arch. I turned left and noticed that the St. Louis Cardinals' Busch Stadium was first on my left. I stopped and talked to an usher who was in the parking lot. He told me where to get the ticket for the arch. Before getting the tickets, I had to solve the problem about where to leave the bike. A stop at the Hyatt and an explanation of what I wanted to do took just five minutes, and soon I left the bike behind safe and sound on my way to get a ticket. Just across the street was the ticket facility inside an old courthouse that faced toward the arch.

Reminded that the Gateway Arch was a National Park Service facility, I bought the ticket and used my national parks pass to reduce the cost of the ticket to $10. Since I was alone, my ticket was for an open time, and the attendant told me to go directly to the line outside the base of the arch. With a wait of about an hour, I was able to get into the interior line where we were divided into groups of five and loaded into cramped tram cars. The ride to the top took about four minutes, then we exited the cars and were allowed into the windowed portion of the arch. The viewing area was very tight and cramped and everyone had to wait their turns to see out the small windows. The views were spectacular, but I think everyone was cramped enough to lessen the enjoyment.

I came back down from the 630-foot-tall arch, the tallest monument in the U.S., and went to a movie about its construction. As is likely while I am on the bike rides, I fell asleep for most of the 20-minute documentary. This has happened all across the country.

The nickname "Gateway City" derived from the days of westward expansion when St. Louis sat on the threshold of unexplored territory. From here in 1804, the Lewis and Clark expedition set out on their two-year-plus exploratory mission into parts unknown.

Back on the streets, I had two things on my mind. I wanted to find someone to give the wallet to and get back on the bike. Neither happened too quickly. No policeman was in sight, so I headed back to the Hyatt and retrieved my bike. The same guys were all gone and another got the bike for me. I hope he shared the tip with the others.

My next goal was to find the Riverfront Trail, a bike and running path along the Mississippi River from St. Louis north. It should have been easy, I thought — just head for the river, not that far away, and I would find the trail. Not that easy. Looking east toward the river, there were constant barricades and one-way streets. I asked a series of folks, and the best response I got was, "I am looking for how to get to the river too!" Two utility workers couldn't help, saying that they got lost in there the week before. A construction guy told me to go back to where I first arrived at the waterfront and find it from there. Finally, I walked into a hotel and asked at the desk, figuring the question had come up before. I got a great attitude and a printout of the streets to follow from the front of the hotel.

Seems like that would have done it, doesn't it? I took off pedaling to follow the directions, but after about four streets ran into another concrete barricade with no way around. I saw a guy walking and asked him to get this response: "Well, the river is right over there. Just head for it." That certainly sounded logical, but I kept riding until there was a hole in the barricades and found myself in a trucking yard of some kind and riding over huge rocks. Finally, I saw a gap ahead and on the other side was a sidewalk that was the Riverfront Trail!

With that problem resolved, I rode north through some of the industrial backside of St. Louis but got some great views of the river, something I always have found very peaceful. The trail continued to very near the Chain of Rocks Bridge, famous for its Route 66 history. Remembering that I still had the found wallet, I spotted a security guard at the county water plant. He gladly accepted the wallet and called the local police while I listened and was told that a car would stop by. I left a business card with him and moved on with that burden passed off to someone else.

I was ready to leave the St. Louis area and wanted to mention a few interesting things before that happened. St. Louis was the home of the first U.S. auto theft in 1905. Two years later, the city became the home of the first gasoline chain, the American Gasoline Company. Most interesting to me was that Charles Lindbergh wanted to name his plane for Lucky Strike cigarettes, but the St. Louis Dispatch stepped in as his principal sponsor, thus the name Spirit of St. Louis.

Just around the corner was the historic bridge, now open only to pedestrians. I rode into the area and read the posters about the great bridge, then rode up onto the mile-long bridge with a bend in the middle. During its heyday, drivers paid a toll to cross the Mississippi River between Granite City, Illinois, and St. Louis. The Chain of Rocks Bridge has wonderful views of the river and was now the second-longest pedestrian bridge in the country.

Once on the Illinois side of the river, there was no state sign, but I already had a record of entering into Illinois at Chester during the 2013 cross-country ride. After a short ride over gradually improving roads, I found my home for the night at the Economy Inn in Granite City, a very small town with several motels, a Hardee's and a convenience store.

My room at the Economy Inn was great, and the WiFi worked just well enough that I could submit my story and pictures to the Post. After a huge meal and milkshake from Hardee's, I had nothing else to explore and eventually went to bed early. Upon rising, I was confident about the day but knew that there were some unknowns coming up.

Out the door about 5:45 a.m., I headed east on Route 66 with a very unusual and slight scraping noise coming from the bike. The noise was so faint that I couldn't be sure just where it originated. The issue confounded me because the bike was fine when I rolled it into the room after the previous day's ride. There were no mechanical problems, and I didn't even have to add air to the tires this morning. Initially, I just kept riding, hoping the problem would go away or give me a clue to the real issue.

At first, I leaned toward the noise possibly coming from the front wheel, yet when I stopped and picked up the frame and spun the front wheel, no sound came forth. I rode on again and realized now that the scraping was getting louder and could be felt through the seat. Afraid that I was damaging the bike, I pulled over and dropped the front wheel out and reattached it. Just a few feet down the road, I knew that my noise was still getting worse. A resident with some knowledge of bikes looked at it and had no idea, but he did remind me that a bike shop was in the next town. Few days on this ride have offered the possibility of a nearby bike shop, but at this point, I was glad one was close today. Totally frustrated, I had more than two hours before the bike shop would open and was determined to find the problem before then and keep my ride going. Just a few miles before Edwardsville, a bike trail crossed my road.

An all-weather shelter sat beside the bike trail and was a good place to get off the bike and ponder the issue. After rolling the bike forward, I found the issue hadn't changed. I pulled the chain and rolled it forward and backward. Everything seemed fine, and I already knew that changing gears didn't do away with the scraping sound.

A new thought came to me to consider the back wheel as the possible culprit and take the time to drop it completely out of the frame and then put it back before I did anything else. Dropping the back wheel was only slightly harder than the front one, so within a couple of minutes, the wheel was back on. The chain was in place and the brakes were reconnected. I hopped on the bike and went for short ride and for the first time all morning heard no noise. I rode in several more gears and all was fine. I reattached the panniers to the bike and headed east with one less concern. The bike ran so quietly that I couldn't believe the simple solution. The wheel must have been in some sort of a bind.

Very soon, I rode into Edwardsville, one of those towns with so many stately older homes that the scenery reminded me of Fulton Street in Salisbury back home. Ready to make up for about an hour of lost time, I pedaled on toward Hamel, a small town significant for two reasons. Sam Parker of Mt. Ulla, not too far down the road from my own farm back in Rowan County, had asked me to stop and visit his friend, Gary Sievers. Gary has a huge farm equipment dealership and has worked with Sam on various occasions. Sam also has family in Hamel. Hamel is also significant to me because the first of my long list of wives has a maiden name of Hamel, and surprisingly, she was born in Chicago, Illinois. My visit with Gary was fun and informative, with me gathering additional insight into the area.

I think I failed to mention that the hills had relaxed when I neared St. Louis, and the same continued on my ride northeast into

Illinois. As suggested by Gary's huge farm equipment inventory, I was now clearly in serious farming country. Gary told me that while most farms would average 2,000 acres, some of the mega-farms could exceed 20,000 acres.

My ride continued into Staunton, where I continued to follow one of the older alignments of Route 66. Slightly disappointed that the road bypassed the downtown area, I soon realized that another good roadside attraction was just ahead. An enterprising person had decided to bury a series of VWs as a parody of the famous Cadillac Ranch near Amarillo, Texas. Not quite as showy and a little less of a draw, only a couple of people were close by at the Route 66 Information Center. I just stopped long enough to take a photo and get back on the bike. There was pedaling to do.

Mt. Olive was the next town whose bright spot was reportedly the oldest remaining Shell service station in the country. Soulsby's Shell Station was operated by the same family from the 1920s until 1991. It was beautifully restored and appeared ready for the next car to pull in to the pumps. I stopped across the street for a fill-up of my own at the very nice convenience store.

Right down the road was Litchfield, the first town of the day that had Route 66 plastered all over it. Litchfield had the Ariston Cafe that has been in continuous operation from the 1920s and also had the nation's longest-running drive-in theater. It apparently had remained a big hit, and the grounds were fantastically manicured. An audio information center was next to the road and was an easy pull-off to hear some of the historical facts of the drive-in. The drive-in first opened in 1950, and the recordings were from some of the first in line and one of the first employees. Reportedly, an evening at the drive-in had consistently topped other local entertainment in attendance.

I passed a series of motels that would have ended my day prematurely in Litchfield, not a hard choice based on information that there were plenty more just ahead. For the last several hours, I had ridden on Route 66 right beside the interstate and was confident that there would be some lodging advertised soon. Gary Sievers had told me to expect plenty of motels in Chatham, but I was informed by two convenience store clerks in Farmerville that there were none. The only motel near Chatham, another of the special older ones, had closed. When I passed it, the closure did not look recent. When asked, another convenience store clerk said, "My God man! You are going to have to ride 45 miles to get a room!" I guess he had no idea how far I had already ridden.

But still there was an unusual happening ahead. I already knew that Illinois was the first state on my journey that did not allow bicycles on the interstate. This fact was plainly posted routinely where I could read it as I pedaled just yards away from the big highway. Remember that I have already stated the fact that bicycles can't ride the interstate!

Very soon, I had to exit Route 66 and head away from the interstate because it was about to cross a big lake without the use of frontage roads. I pedaled into some beautiful farming country in search of a bike trail that would give me access to cross the lake and deliver me into Springfield, Illinois. This route was a good one with almost no traffic, but it was circuitous and added extra miles for cyclists with no other choice.

I found the bike trail in Chatham and pedaled east along a well-kept greenway with a railroad track beside me. Train after train came rolling by, one of them pulled by a Norfolk Southern engine. Those trains were closer than the big trucks had been on I-55. I saw a lady fall from her bike and hit her head, but she seemed to be OK and was close to home. Her husband gave me a few pointers, one of them stating that the nearest motels were all the chain types and very expensive.

After leaving the bike trail, I pedaled on to finally access the city and quickly rolled in to the nearest convenience store. Needing some help with the best plan, I asked at the store for reasonable motels close by and the clerk pointed to her right and told me that a Motel 6 was just an exit away. That was great news to me because the day had already been a long one. Oddly enough, I did not know and didn't much care what the road directly in front of the store was. I knew it had a lot of traffic, but the access was to simply turn right onto it. After riding just less than three miles and already on my exit, I heard a siren behind me and realized that I had been pulled over for the second time ever on a bike.

I stopped and looked at the Illinois State Trooper who told me to stay on the bike while he put his hat on. Once he left the car, he started talking about the fact that bicycles were not legal on interstates in Illinois. Then he said the same thing two more times! I showed him my map and explained that I had just entered this road and was already in the process of my exit toward the motel. I even showed him a coupon for a discounted motel price that was good for today. By now, I knew it was wrong to be on this road but I was not sure that I wouldn't have done it again had the road been identified better. The trooper took my license and proceeded to sit in his car for the next 20 minutes while I paced around my bike that was now leaning against a reflector post. Finally, he emerged to tell me that I was free to go, but still issued a warning ticket. Should I be caught on the Illinois interstate again, I would be charged! Then he said, "You may not know it but Route 66 is no longer continuous and you will have to finish the rest of your journey without riding on the interstate." I showed my map again and he realized that the map agreed with him. Finally, he let me go and I pedaled another quarter of a mile to the Motel 6.

Today had been spectacular weatherwise with little wind, cooler temperatures and not a threat of rain. The terrain had been as good as any on the trip, but still it had been a long day. The day's mileage totaled 96 and left me about 220 miles to reach Chicago. I had a blast today!

My evening in Springfield was mostly a good one. I walked to the McDonald's and brought back plenty of breakfast items for dinner again. They gave me extra water so I didn't need a convenience store visit and planned to do that early the next morning on the way to the Lincoln sites. My Motel 6 room was fine, except when a neighbor decided to air a nasty phone call in the hall next to my door. I went to the door to "ssshhhh" her and it worked. This was a new and very basic Motel 6. For the second time on this trip, I got the handicapped room and I am unsure of what that means. I could have stored the bike, or even ten of them, in the bathroom!

After another good night's sleep, and it seems like nearly all of them are while on the road, I stopped by the desk for suggestions as to how to find the Lincoln sites. Abraham Lincoln spent most of his life in Springfield, Illinois, and I have continued to be a huge fan of Lincoln history. I was about to hit the jackpot, as much as my brief time and bicycle would allow. The clerk gave me a small map to aid in my tour of the city but was not sure of the specifics of each location and which ones might be the best to see.

After leaving the motel, I refueled and reloaded at the convenience store across from McDonald's. This clerk didn't know much either but was huge fun to talk with so early in the morning. A little flirting possibly went on, which was fine with me. For the first time in my life, I bought one of those high-priced bananas from the basket at the checkout.

The time came to get serious, and I was back on the bike headed for downtown Springfield. In another "blind hog finding an acorn" story, and before I realized it, I was back on Route 66. I thought to myself, "Can this be right? Am I even headed in the right direction?" I not only found myself on the correct route but realized that Route 66 ran near "Lincoln's Neighborhood," a national park and the actual area where Abraham Lincoln lived during his time in the city. His home, the only one he ever owned, and many of the other surrounding homes have been renovated to their pre-Civil War appearance. It was a beautiful and somber place on this early Sunday morning amidst these homes from 1860.

Also, nearby was the Illinois State Capitol Building that Lincoln used for several of his speeches and debates. His statue stands in front of the magnificent building where the president's body lay in state following his assassination. Most moving to me was the depot where Lincoln gave his last speech to the residents of Springfield before heading off to Washington as president of the United States. Part of that speech reads, "Who knows when and if I may ever return," and of course he did not return alive.

Right on track as the sun continued its rise on this beautiful Sunday morning, I stopped briefly at a McDonald's nearby for breakfast and then pedaled toward Williamsville. The main entrance to Williamsville was blocked for railroad work, and there was not even room for me to walk the bicycle around the area. With a huge storm building to the west, I retraced my track back to the edge of the town and rejoined Route 66, which was now headed more northerly than before. A sign said that the Route 66 frontage road was closed at 60th Street, which meant nothing to me. I was already out of Williamsville and no other towns were nearby. I continued to pedal ahead of the building storm that now included some distant lightning.

By now, it was apparent that there were no other vehicles on the road. If there was a road closure ahead, I hoped that my continued luck in these situations would hold enough to let me get around it. With rain now imminent, I found the road closure and two workers already sitting in their truck even before it rained. I waved to them as I pedaled by on the dirt surface, but they didn't take time to return a friendly gesture.

Minutes later and now past the road closure, I felt the first rain drops and knew that many more would follow. But once again, I didn't take out my unused rain jacket. Suddenly, a torrential downpour hit, complete with lightning and nearby thunder, slamming me just as I rode into Elkhart. Another cyclist, Bill Peterman of Sherman, was already under a downtown store roof and made great company while we waited out the storm. Bill, a triathlete currently, was interested in my ride and told me that he had plans to do something similar in the future. Bill had called his wife to come pick him up and soon as the heavy rain let up, I was back on the road. Almost as soon as I returned to 66, the heavy rain hit again but there was no reason to stop pedaling.

Nobody noticed as I passed through Broadwell with little fanfare and then rode into Lincoln. Lincoln, of course, was named for then still alive President Lincoln to which he later said, "I never knew of anything named Lincoln that amounted to much." The Route 66 landmark in town was "The Mill," a 1920s eatery that had a revolving windmill with lights during its heyday. After being closed for many years, there was an ongoing effort to restore the building as a museum.

By now, the rain had passed, and I pedaled uphill toward Atlanta where the 1930s Palms Café was doing a brisk business on a Sunday afternoon. I stopped to get two slices of their best pie in an effort to continue my tradition as unofficial pie tester at the old Route 66 cafes. The giant "Hot Dog Man" was right across the street and continued to provide lots of photo opportunities. Atlanta also had an eight-sided library that Mr. Lincoln actually visited.

The next towns were McLean, Funk's Grove and Shirley with little reason to stop. Not much of a syrup user, I did consider stopping near Funk's Grove to pick up some of the Funk family "sirup" but decided to pass on by. The Sunday afternoon wind was blowing hard as a tailwind for me. "Never waste a tailwind" remained a favorite motto of mine.

The Bloomington-Normal area was my intended stop for the evening, and I had already called ahead to a suggested Super 8 Motel and predicted a 3 p.m. arrival. A little unsure of where Bloomington ended and Normal started, I stopped for directions and was told to just keep pedaling through Bloomington and the same Main Street would then become Normal.

Bloomington is a college town and certainly has the look of one with varying degrees of trendiness and quirkiness. The large football stadium of Illinois State University bumped against Main Street. Bloomington also seemed to go on forever with plenty of stoplights and hills. I was afraid that there might be a checkpoint that would only allow those visitors without issues into Normal, but none existed. My Super 8 appeared finally after an unusual 78 miles for the day. The good news was another Denny's next door and the bad was a very serious hazardous weather forecast for the night. High humidity seemed to already be encouraging another storm, but none appeared in the area as I rolled my bike to an inside room.

As mentioned often before, I love Sunday rides. Less traffic and the more relaxed pace of those who are on the road made for another less-frenzied day. For once, I was fine being an hour late. I had closed the distance to Chicago, which was now about 150 miles to the north.

I woke up in the Super 8 room and was immediately treated to a fireworks show out the window. The predicted overnight storms had not been as harsh as expected but were still in the area. Light rain was falling, but according to the weather reports, the worst of the rain had begun to move out of the area. It was tempting just to lie in bed and watch the storm, but more riding beckoned and Chicago was just around the corner.

To find the Super 8 the previous evening, I rode off course and needed to reconnect quickly that morning. I studied my map and phone after consulting the motel manager. I went to bed with a plan that seemed right for a quick return to Route 66. I wanted to get on Shelbourne Street and head for the town of Towanda. After stumbling onto Towanda Avenue, I took it and soon found that I had ridden the wrong way and still had to access Shelbourne to rejoin 66. After a couple of wrong-way miles, I found Shelbourne only to discover that the road was closed to all traffic, including bikes. Right beside the street was a freshly paved pedestrian greenway, but it was closed, too. Since it was important to reacquire Route 66, I rode around the road closed signs. By now, no one reading this book should be surprised.

About two miles into the greenway, I found it and the road both completely blocked where some drainage work was being done. I decided to drag the bike through a swampy area and was soon back on the other side of the greenway. An early arriving worker sat in his car as I passed, but he never looked up from his phone. For several miles, I had the road to myself since it was blocked from the other end, too. The bike path continued on and eventually used a paved-over portion of the older Route 66 lanes, now no longer needed for cars. Some portions of this greenway were also blocked for no apparent reason, and since the greenway was better than the road, I pedaled around the barriers yet again.

Since this long adventure began in California, I have seen the famous Burma Shave quotes often along the way. Burma Shave broke a poem or extended phrase into about six signed segments with a moral at the end and definitely grabbed the attention of this cyclist as I rode past them.

The next town was definitely one of my favorites for various reasons. Pontiac was so proud of its Route 66 connection and of its history, too. I took time to ride completely around the downtown and spotted a few special things. Pontiac was centered around another majestic courthouse that was still in everyday use since the time of Abraham Lincoln himself. Lincoln served the area as a circuit court judge, traveling by horseback. Another Lincoln statue stood in front of the entrance.

Other interesting sites included a series of painted storefronts that depicted life during the heyday of Route 66. The town had a Route 66 Museum, just outside of which was parked the modified school bus that famous 66 painter and photographer Bob Waldmire used for his travels. The bus, often described as a land yacht, was amazing to see. Waldmire lived in it for months at a time. Pontiac also has little "Cars" cutouts from the Pixar movie on every street corner complete with individual themes. With a cooling light rain still falling through the morning, my tour of Pontiac was very enjoyable.

On to Odell, another town that had an underground passageway so that pedestrians could safely cross beneath the busy Route 66 traffic. Odell also had a restored Standard service station that now served as the town's visitor center. The next town was Dwight, with probably the best restored and most interesting of all the old gas stations along my way. The Ambler-Becker Texaco Station was used continuously from 1933 to 1999, making it the record holder for all of Route 66. This station also served as the visitor center for the area and was manned by two extraordinary ladies when I stopped by. They urged me to see the rest of the town, but rail construction for future high-speed use had most of the area completely blocked, severely hampering close-up views of the major historical attractions. Traffic was terrible in the construction area, and I chose to make better use of my time heading east, so I waved to the two ladies as I passed by again on the way out of town.

Often, I have been surprised by the quality of things seen in a very small downtown area. Such was the case in Gardner. My first stop was to visit the local post office to send a package home for the purpose of making space in my bags. Postmaster Debbie Richards was a lot of fun as she helped me complete the mailing of the package and then joined me for a series of photos in front of her building. After leaving the post office, I continued on Route 66 to find a two-cell jail that was used in the early 1900s and an old bus restored to the Route 66-era diner that it once was.

I followed the 66 symbols and arrows on the road to exit the town and immediately was confused on the proper road choice. After briefly making the wrong choice, I tried a U-turn and tumbled off the bike. With the weight carried on the bike, tight turns are always best avoided, and this was another prime reminder of that fact. The only bad result was a bloody elbow that belonged to the embarrassed rider.

Braceville was next on the way to Braidwood. I was told the previous night that a shortage of available rooms existed in Braidwood due to two festivals in the area. I did find a motel, and hoped I could make it through the night without any issues. After 80 miles on another warm afternoon, I only had the choice of food at a convenience store. The store was nice with lots of selections, but my debit card was declined twice for payment, forcing me to use a credit card instead. This has happened often because banks have certain triggers for fraudulent use of cards and frequent travel between states for repeated purchases has been one of them.

With my food in hand, I headed back to the motel, hoping that enough things in the room would work to provide a restful night. It was closely akin to camping in a motel. When I first entered the motel, it seemed more of a long-term residence facility. Half the lights in my room didn't work and the toilet wasn't much better. Nothing was extra clean and the towels were small and thin. I had to ask for plastic cups and a few cigarette burns adorned the best chair. But the success of the day was not linked to the motel room. Today's most enjoyable features were the wonderful people, fantastic scenery, far-ahead views of the grain elevators, crickets that chirped during the rain and endless passenger trains that flew by.

The night at the Sun Motel passed uneventfully and there were some positives. The room was quiet and the bed was good, there was plenty of ice plus the WiFi worked great throughout. Enough said, but I was glad to move on. With each great adventure, there has been a mixture of lots of good along with a little bad, or as I preferred to say, a little less good.

Right out the door, I headed back over toward Route 66 and my exit from Braidwood. But before I did, I had to see the Polk-A-Dot Drive-In that has been in business since the 1950s. Elvis had two statues outside and Marilyn Monroe, James Dean and Betty Boop had one each.

An easy and early morning ride along State Road 53 took me to Wilmington, a town divided by the magnificent Kankakee River. The Kankakee was one of the prettiest along Route 66. Another attraction that I looked for was the Gemini Giant. Afraid that I had missed it just as the edge of town came in sight, I stopped to ask a resident who was walking nearby. Our conversation was fun as I told him briefly about my ride. The Gemini Giant was just a couple of blocks ahead, where he stood holding a rocket and wearing what I thought was an astronaut's helmet. The Giant has been used in almost as many marketing photos as the Blue Whale.

Next was the very small Elmwood on the left side of Route 66 as I pedaled toward Joliet. Up ahead on my right was a huge structure that looked more and more like a racetrack. I was surprised to find the Chicagoland Speedway and the smaller Route 66 Speedway, just as I had found the Kentucky Speedway on last year's Underground Railroad adventure. Always at least a moderate NASCAR fan, I had been oblivious that Route 66 had a major racetrack, especially since Chicago was still at least 50 miles away.

After I finally arrived in Joliet along with plenty of heavy traffic, the road ahead was especially confusing. Route 66 continued ahead, but my map called for a turn that was blocked by signs adjacent to a police station. Probably not the best place to go around these signs, I rode on ahead and got directions from two meter readers. I had to go back down the street and go around the signs because the desired road was only open to pedestrians.

I found the Plank Road Trail and rode on it for 22 miles, briefly used the streets of Chicago Heights and worked to find the Thorn Creek Trail. I found what I thought was the trail and followed it, and became more confused. The trail was not labeled and it crossed another trail, so I stopped to get help from the patrons of a local bar. My goal was Lansing, a perfect gateway to Chicago for me. All the trail riding for this day was considered by the authors of my cycling map a safer alternative to enter Chicago than riding some of the streets.

On a personal note, the first Dairy Queen was established here in 1940. I wondered if the first store had my favorite pineapple milkshakes.

Some of that heavy traffic was in Lansing, just less than 30 miles from waterfront Chicago. On my way to the Star Way Inn, another recommended motel, I stopped at Walmart for some food and a new red flashing light. My other one was lost off the back of the bike the day before. Much of the heavy traffic seemed to follow me into and out of the parking lot.

The motel was actually part of the same complex and just a long parking lot away. With the day completed, I looked forward to the final ride to Chicago the next morning. My plans included an extended ride afterwards, but first I wanted to close out Route 66 in a big way.

CHAPTER (11)

Chicago, my kind of town;
Bonus riding, Indiana to Michigan and back again

Every day had started with a dose of excitement for me since this ride began. But this very morning, July 20, 2016, provided at least a double dose. I was excited and ready to go to Chicago, experience one of the greatest cities in the world on a bike and then see what the rest of the day would hold.

I was confident that I could make it to Chicago from Lansing by mid-morning, even though I had to travel during rush hour. Previous trips to the Windy City had acquainted me with the area, but this entry route was different. I consulted the maps the previous night and felt very confident.

From Lansing, with about 25 miles to ride, I pedaled on in the early dawn light to Calumet City and then Burnham. These were suburbs of Chicago that had little definition of where one city ended and the next one started. A freight train blocked the street for about 20 minutes in Burnham, where I listened to a few of the drivers say that there was not a good alternative. Still, many of them turned around while I sat about as patiently as possible, hoping that the train would move soon. One driver chose to take out his frustration verbally on me once we started rolling again, something that didn't bother me at all. I had nothing to do with his wait and quickly discounted his harsh words. The driver asked me rather tersely to get on the sidewalk, which just happened to end as soon as we cleared the railroad track. I wondered if the driver noticed that, too.

My first sight of Lake Michigan was my short-term goal, but I knew that there would still be a long ride to the city afterwards. After the city streets of the suburbs, I finally arrived at Lake Shore Drive with its nice bike lanes and then, eventually, bike paths. Hundreds of cyclists were using Lake Shore that morning for workouts or for commuting to work. One of those commuters caught up to me and said, "So, where are you going?" Thus began a very pleasant seven-mile conversation with Hilary Haselton, one of those long-time bicycle commuters.

Hilary had been an advertising copywriter for about 15 years and had pedaled into the city many of those mornings. During our ride, we discussed lots of topics and briefly described what brought us both to be here on this summer morning. As the city's tall buildings came nearer, Hilary and I talked about the ceremonial end of my ride. Grant Park's Buckingham Fountain, or as close as we could get while still on the bike path, was the end of our ride together. We made pictures and vowed to stay in touch while Hilary asked that I let her know when I would be in Chicago again.

With that, Hilary headed for work, and I began to make my way over to the fountain. My trips to Chicago before had included visiting my daughter, running a half marathon and a few times on business. Amber went to broadcasting school for a year here. I had seen the fountain before but couldn't wait to see it up close again, particularly on this day. With a big festival coming up called Lollapalooza, the park was essentially under construction on this morning, and many of the entrances were blocked, but pedestrians were finding ways around the fencing, and so did I. The beautiful fountain looked great on this special morning while bringing back memories of the opening of "Married With Children."

Another unique part of this day was my meeting with an adventurer named Rasheed Hooda. Rasheed planned to walk Route 66 backwards, starting that same afternoon. I said backwards because he planned to walk east to west, opposite of what I did. Rasheed had found the chronicles of my travels online and had contacted me about three weeks before with a desire to meet in Chicago if possible. Our messages to each other on this day had consisted of narrowing down the time to meet after he arrived by bus and I did by bike.

I found Rasheed near the fountain, and we talked like old friends about my ride and what he planned to do. Rasheed expected to take five to six months to complete his journey to Santa Monica. We both walked over to the official street signs for the start and end of Route 66 and made pictures at both. The signs were on Jackson and Adams streets, not far from the waterfront. In the early days of Route 66, one street served as both the start and end, but the alignment was changed in later years due to the advent of one-way streets.

Hilary had suggested a celebratory donut at DoRite Donuts on nearby Randolph Street, so Rasheed and I headed there to continue our discussion. Not your everyday donuts, these were huge and just under $3 each. Mine was a cheese Danish donut, chosen after I noted the continuous demand from the real Chicagoans. DoRite Donuts was only a very small hole in the wall, but the line never seemed to end for the high-priced treats.

As we ate, Rasheed asked me questions about what to expect on his soon-to-begin journey. Rasheed had arranged for his nephew to pick him up after his walks for each of the next three days. They planned to return to the nephew's home for food and a good night's sleep before returning to the previous day's end point. I felt as if I had found an old friend and was completely comfortable in his presence. Rasheed planned to start walking around noon, and I left him to visit a McDonald's for last-minute food and phone charging while I found a 7-Eleven and restocked my bags.

Completely assured that there was no real hurry for my departure, I walked the bike back through the park and over to the waterfront. Lake Michigan was just as beautiful as any of the other Great Lakes, and I took time to sit and observe the people and the scenery of this fast-moving place. Runners, walkers and cyclists kept the waterfront area busy on what turned out to be one of the best weather days since leaving California. I had all those pleasant memories from the other trips to Chicago, and it was worth taking a few minutes to revisit them.

Finally, at just before 3 p.m., I decided to head back southwest for the first time. All of my sustained riding had been directly east from the start and then had gradually turned northeast for the final entrance into Chicago. Never planning too far ahead, I also decided this morning to head back to Lansing for another night and use it for a launching pad toward bonus riding eastward into Indiana and Michigan. My cycling journeys had yet to include Michigan, and I was close enough to visit the state this time. Past that, I had tentative plans to be picked up by car for the return to North Carolina.

The Great Lakes have each appealed to me since my first sight of Lake Erie from the bicycle seat last summer, and Chicago has been the largest city overlooking one. Similar to Toronto, Chicago seemed energized by the huge expanse of open water. I hated to leave the city and the great waterfront, but it was time to go. It was a sad goodbye, but there was pedaling to do!

The ride back to Lansing was uneventful, except that I tried to use the trail system even more than on the morning trip. Traffic never became an issue, no trains blocked my progress and I suspected that my return trip was faster. This time, I entered Lansing with a little more confidence than the first time when I was unsure of the proper route. I rode into the same area but this time went directly toward the Red Roof Inn. The sign said, "Rooms, $39.95 and up." It sounded too good to be true, and as is usually the case, it was. My quoted rate was significantly higher, and the clerk added an extra charge for a refrigerator and microwave. I was told that the low rate was only for Ford employees who stay at the motel for seven or more days. She finally admitted that this rate was seldom used, if in fact it ever had been. We settled on a more reasonable rate and no additional charges for the microwave and refrigerator.

My first stop once the bike was in the room was to visit the next-door IHOP, the real drawing card of the Red Roof Inn. I wanted to see if IHOP could somehow compete with the great meals received along the way at Denny's. Not quite the same volume of food was a disappointment, but for sure everything tasted great. Denny's had larger pancakes and a bigger order of scrambled eggs and I got hash browns without an extra charge. IHOP did match the two large waters for a big plus in their corner. I took all of it back to the room and put my feet up with maps spread out on the bed.

After asking at the desk about the nearest convenience store, I later walked down the sidewalk in my sandals to find it. I bought four different kinds of waters and drinks and knew that I would consume it all. A quick stop at Wendy's was good for another Frosty.

Now with the final days of this ride approaching, I looked forward to the challenge of finding my way without any semblance of a planned route. I had Mapquest, Google and an Illinois map to start. Indiana was very close by, and I needed its printed map and probably would need a Michigan map, too. My history in these situations has been just to wing it, not the best way to proceed, but usually it worked out somehow. It looked like the completion of the bonus riding would come Saturday afternoon, somewhere in Indiana.

After finishing my 35-day journey on Route 66 that morning,

I was convinced that "America's Highway" was my favorite journey to date. I felt an ever-growing kinship with all those who have traveled the famous highway before. A lot of brave souls pushed America's boundaries and helped make our great nation what it is today. Conquering the heat played a part, too.

The Mapquest route was mind-boggling, with 80 turns over 93 miles. I did not yet have an Indiana map but looked at a map on my iPad where Ridge Road seemed to be the best way to begin the journey toward Michigan. My first goal was East Chicago, the best place to begin to follow Route 12 up the Lake Michigan coast. Route 41 was my planned connector from Ridge Road to Route 12, but it was very busy as rush hour was building. I saw a policeman who had parked to clock traffic and asked him what he thought of my planned route. The policeman was very personable and in great shape, and we talked about my bike ride. He gave his approval, saying he didn't know of a better route and that the traffic would thin out after I passed the expressway just ahead.

I rode into East Chicago, now with an Indiana map in hand just in case. East Chicago was in Indiana but still had lots of commuter trains heading into Chicago, Illinois. Hilary from Chicago had told me how ethnically diverse East Chicago was, and I saw signs of that. Route 41 took me to Route 12 east, and I headed east close enough to Lake Michigan to see gulls flying but with no sight of the water.

Just past East Chicago was Gary, Indiana, probably the worst-looking American city that I have seen. Burned-out buildings, boarded-up houses and plenty of trash dominated the scenery on this morning. Almost every building that still had an operating business in it displayed bars on the windows and doors. I was very glad to pedal out of town. Afterwards came miles and miles of large steel mills to my left toward the water. I still had not seen any of

Lake Michigan on this morning. Huge trucks, running to and from the steel mills, kept me on my toes. This was not the beautiful area that I had hoped it would be.

The highlight of the morning was a stop at the Indiana Dunes National Seashore. With my national parks pass at the ready, I rode up to the guardhouse. The ranger told me that all cyclists were free but to watch out for pedestrians walking from the parking lot to the beach area. In my opinion, the idea of a free pass for cyclists was a spectacular boost for all parks. I remained a big fan of the $10 national parks pass, too. I rode about a mile to see the dunes, most of them grown over with foliage. A huge concrete and brick beach house was the gateway to those who planned to spend time near the water. I got my first look at Lake Michigan from the seashore in Indiana and enjoyed it tremendously. After a few pictures, I got back on the bike and rode out of the park and headed east again on Route 12. Just as I turned on 12, I saw another very heavy-laden cyclist pedal toward me.

Expecting to share some information, I crossed the road and waited on him. I think the rider was French or possibly Canadian, but I couldn't understand anything that he said except that he had ridden the train for part of his journey. I eventually wished him well with nothing worthwhile exchanged between us.

Farther north, I joined again with the National Seashore, this part dotted with plenty of beach houses. I was amazed to see that so many of them looked as if they were uninhabited. Some of the yards had grass several feet high, so the big mystery for me was what had happened to the owners. These views were spectacular, and most of the houses were on the high bank to my right.

After leaving the waterfront area, I pedaled away from the sea-shore on a very rough road amid an onslaught of horseflies, worse than anything I had ever seen. I couldn't ride fast enough or slap at them in time to get away. Then, just as suddenly, they were gone. After escaping the large flies, a huge storm closed in from the west with extreme winds. Michigan City, oddly still in Indiana, was my next town. Some hills had again appeared as the storm threatened. I buttoned up my bags in preparation for the impending storm.

Nothing more than drizzle fell as the winds settled. I had planned to ride on for another 20 miles or so, but noticed a small motel on my right as I pedaled north. At first, I discounted the motel because there were no stores close by. But just a little more than a mile past the Buffalo Motel, I realized that New Buffalo was in fact a quaint and interesting town with plenty of stores including a grocery. Still, I rode on until I saw the highway turn dead east away from the water. I decided to retrace my route and call the motel. The owner told me she had one room at a very reasonable price, and I decided to call it a day after 66 trying miles.

I did stop at a little hydroponic, or water gardening, shop just before calling and turning around for sure. No one besides the owner was in the shop and he acted as if it was a tremendous bother to look up the name of the small motel that I had passed. Finally, the owner said, "Look, I don't know where the phone book is, and I don't know of any motel on the other side of town." I took the hint and headed back out to find the number on my phone and was glad to reach a very pleasant motel owner.

The Buffalo Motel was perfect, very stylish and even had chocolate seashell candies for my room. I submitted my story for the day and headed back to town and the harbor where the motel owner told me to wait for the sunset over the water. I stopped at the amazing grocery where the employees were freshly preparing lots of food in the store. I bought a bag full of fruit, yogurt, custard and a veggie sandwich and walked the bike through an evening farmers market complete with entertainment. The beautiful harbor was just ahead, and it was time for wheel dipping and eating. Plenty of others walked along the harbor waiting for the sunset that was certainly in doubt. The clouds lingered, and the sun had not appeared. I got several photos of my front wheel dipped in Lake Michigan and waited for a possible break in the clouds. None came, and I headed back for the room and what probably was going to be my last night on the road.

New Buffalo was about as quaint as one of the Maine towns that I loved so much a couple of summers before. I promised myself a return visit because there was more to see. I left the motel the next morning with nature in make-up mode. I pedaled toward one of the most spectacular sunrises I had ever seen, and this one lingered longer than normal. My east-bound journey had yielded a dozen or so sunrises of note but nothing that matched this one. Amazing colors filled the sky.

On I rode to Three Oaks, the only real town of the morning. I was back in farming country, but the traffic again kept me focused along with on again, off again shoulders. A well-stocked and very busy convenience store helped me reload my bags, and for the first time, I saw a credit card air machine. There was also a cyclist sculpture across the road.

Just east of Three Oaks were more beautiful farms as my mind became focused on a visit to South Bend and Notre Dame. I found my way into the campus and quickly spotted the famous gold dome. I rode toward it. Not sure exactly where I could ride the bike, I stopped and asked a professor for some tips. He told me how to find the football stadium and "Football Jesus," a huge mural that faces the stadium, and the Knute Rockne statue. That statue stood just outside the players' tunnel, where I could see just a small portion of the field.

Multiple parents' tours were going on around the main part of campus. I listened to one guide who told his group, "Let's walk over here near the Knute Rockne statue and we can see a small portion of the field. They won't let me take you out to the field, but I wish I could." I found it odd that the field was so sacred that the parents of prospective students couldn't get a view of the field, either from the stands or better yet from one of the end zones.

Mapquest directions got me back on track to leave the campus and head south out of town. My route continued south on what I thought was the best and safest route possible. On yet another hot day, I passed through endless stoplights before finally connecting with Route 35. The stoplights were a forgotten issue as the road became an expressway, and I saw the dreaded sign that said pedestrians and bicycles were prohibited. Not sure of another route, I continued to ride the expressway for about ten miles before exiting just ahead of a policeman entering on the northbound side.

I sat for a while at the bottom of the exit ramp wondering how to proceed and thought I had made sense of the predicament by using the Indiana map again. I decided to head toward Bremen, Indiana, and figure out from there where to spend the night. The highlight of the late afternoon was more fantastic farming country, but the issue was that the roads didn't have shoulders. My only stop for directions came when I saw a woman in front of her house. She confirmed that I was on the right road, so I battled traffic and eventually found myself on Main Street in Bremen. I inquired about the listed motel in town and was told that it was just ahead on Main Street.

What followed, on my last night on the road, was the most unusual motel experience of the trip. I found the motel easily enough, but it didn't look quite right. I had called a few times earlier and got no answer, reminding me of earlier experiences that sometimes found the motel closed. I knocked on the door of the office and went in. Nobody was in the office but the phone had a display that said "79 messages," which certainly made me wonder what had happened. The house next door was connected to the end of the motel so I went there and knocked on the door. A young mother with a baby answered the door and asked if she could help me. I said simply, "Are you open? I am looking for a room." The young mother told a man watching TV to help me, and he came outside just before the plot got thicker.

The owner told me that he was sold out and that the nearest motel was about 20 miles to the south. The afternoon was getting late, and the temperature was still near 100, so I asked, "Do you not have anything?" He told me that two rooms were being remodeled but were not ready for renting. He finally did agree to show me the rooms and allowed me to pick the simpler and less torn up of the rooms. I was glad to get it after 64 challenging miles.

Oddly, the owner had to get me a pillowcase and some towels and then he left the motel. I unloaded a few things and turned the AC unit on before riding back to the nearby Dairy Queen for my last pineapple milkshake. I got to celebrate the last night on the road with a restaurant full of Amish and Mennonite families. One of the families questioned me about my ride, and it was interesting to talk with them. The dad started the conversation and then called his family over and they told me that bicycles were an everyday mode of transportation for them around Bremen.

I then stopped at the McDonald's next door for an evening breakfast before returning to the room. While there, the only other customer began a conversation about where I was from. He told me that his girlfriend was in the hospital after a bad fall and he just had to get out of the place for a good meal. I promised to pray for his girlfriend and asked if he was going back there tonight. The reply was something like, "Yes, I suppose I will have to take her some food, too!"

When I arrived back at the room, the air temperature outside was still in the high 90s, and the air in the room was not far behind. The AC unit was not cooling, and I knew that I was out of options. It would be a warm night but a good shower eventually helped me to sleep, although very fitfully. I prayed for rest as the long night drew on. I had no WiFi, and neither did the nearby Dairy Queen, but the always reliable McDonald's had me covered. Other than the great shower, it was a night with few amenities that slowly drug out my last motel stay of this adventure.

As you might have guessed, I was up early and ready to ride. My route for the day looked to be very rural, and since today was a Saturday, I hoped for moderate traffic. I rode out of Bremen to the south where few cars were moving once I reached another round of the beautiful farmland. A low-lying fog blanketed the fields early as the dawn was breaking, another welcome add-on. I need not have worried about the traffic. The early risers gave me plenty of room, so I was free to enjoy the scenery.

A few things contributed to the enjoyment of my final day of riding. At a higher rate than normal, people threw up their hands to wave as we met on the road or as I pedaled by. Good shoulders and cooler-than-expected early temperatures hit the spot, too. State Roads 331, 25 and 35 were perfect choices, a fact that amazed me. Route 35 was the same road considered an expressway just a day earlier, but not so on this day. I kicked myself for not just staying on the expressway a little farther and probably finding a motel with working AC. In retrospect, it was all just a part of the experience, during which I certainly have had worse.

Now that I rode directly south, my shadow pedaled along easily on my right. Only a few times had I seen my shadow on this ride, but today it consistently kept up, often looking more effortless than expected. There was plenty of time for retrospective thought as I pedaled through the small towns of Bourbon, Rochester and Logansport. All were beautiful in their own way with lots of older homes, many of which were wonderfully restored. Historic-looking downtowns, always my favorites, were just what I wanted to see.

Two other very small towns caught my eye, too. Tippecanoe and Talma were unique in their own ways. Talma had a historical marker recording the fact that no other town in the United States claimed the same name. Tippecanoe was close to the site of a battle between U.S. soldiers and the Shawnee Indians. The U.S. general was William Henry Harrison, who later used the term, "Tippecanoe and Tyler too" during the presidential election of 1840.

Another historical marker caught my eye later. The Potawatomie Indian Tribe was sent on its own Trail of Tears in 1838. The marker recognized the site of the first Indian child's death as the tribe was forced to march from Indiana to Kansas. Many of them did not survive their own perilous journey.

My next and last town of the whole adventure was Walton, Indiana. The end of my ride that now totaled 38 days and 2,778 miles was at hand. My nephew, Sammy Freeze, pulled his SUV into a Marathon convenience store at 2 p.m., and we proceeded to load the bike into the back of the vehicle. Sammy had driven from near China Grove, North Carolina, since early that morning, and Walton was the perfect meeting place. I changed clothes, grabbed a little bit of food and prepared for the long car ride home.

The bike and I were both fine. The day played out as the perfect last day for my extended Route 66 journey. My mileage for the day was a very appropriate 66 miles. I will look back on the long journey in the next chapter.

CHAPTER ⑫

For several reasons, I was drawn to ride the entire length of Route 66. But there were a few reasons not to, especially during the heat of summer. I began planning the odyssey months before with the choice of whether to ride through the Mojave Desert or the much cooler northwestern states of Washington on to the Dakotas and into Minnesota and Wisconsin.

Over the last four years, my summertime cycling adventures have been rewarding in a manner that I couldn't have expected. Such was the case with this one. A total of 2,778 miles over 38 days, part of it in the hottest temperatures I had ever experienced. The concern for the heat was well founded and played out with a high official temperature of 117 degrees in Kingman, Arizona, with Oatman, Arizona, and Needles, California, not far behind.

The heat was certainly formidable but still bearable. Only on the long uphill ride to Oatman did I suffer, and a proper decision to take the afternoon off on that day settled the issue. Under doctor's orders this time to be serious about my hydration, I carried more water and used it. The extreme dry mouth which had been a symptom of severe dehydration in the past just didn't happen. At times, my panniers were jammed with more water than I had ever carried before, and on one occasion, there was just enough.

I was reminded of the old science experiment when a frog was put in a pan of warm water. As the water was slowly brought to a boil, the frog never jumped back out. Yet, if the frog was put into a pot of already boiling water, he jumped right out immediately. Something similar must have happened to me. Most morning temperatures were at least reasonable, and I started off just fine. As the midday and afternoon temperatures climbed, I just stayed on the bike and kept riding. The slow warm-up didn't seem so bad.

The hills had been a concern, too; not so much because they were extreme but because hills and heat together made a much bigger challenge. The Rockies in 2013 were much higher than the 7,000-plus feet that was the crest of Route 66. Looking back, the climbing was a constant but nothing remarkable. The Ozarks are still the hardest climbing I have experienced on the bike, and this was my second battle with them.

Weather conditions otherwise turned out to be quite moderate. As expected, there was little rain. I never removed my rain jacket from the pannier even though there were several times of severe thunderstorms. Any rain at first was welcomed for the cooling effects, so I just rode with wet clothing. In retrospect, the storm as I neared Rolla would have been the best time to use the jacket. Regardless, the jacket has plenty of wear remaining for the next ride.

No serious bike problems caused any real concern along the way even though I was certainly perplexed with the scraping noise on the first morning in Illinois. Two flats and the scraping issue were minimal concerns, and again I was very happy with the Surly bike. My flats still averaged less than one per 1,000 miles. The answer for the question I'm most often asked remained the same from previous rides. The bike seat did not bother me, even on a 12-hour day on the bike. I continued the use of some anti-abrasion lubricant early in the ride, and no issues followed. The saga of the flashing taillight was ongoing, and I found that the best one came from Walmart.

Before I leave the subject of flat tires, it's worth revisiting that storm just ahead of Rolla one more time. With miles to go before I could reach safety in the worst wind, rain and visibility of the whole journey, I prayed for the back tire to hold enough air to avoid the flat in such extreme conditions. My prayers, as yet another true example of how God rides with me, were answered. I can't express how unlikely that scenario was. Every single flat that I had otherwise over 13,000 miles happened quickly. This one held enough air for approximately 45 minutes after I noticed the leak, an incredible time for a slow leak with a rider on board. Because the air held, I was able to reach shelter during a storm that caused extensive wind and erosion damage throughout the area. This was simply an amazing blessing as the tire went completely flat within 10 minutes after I reached the Econo Lodge.

These concerns were more up front than ongoing during the ride. My only close call during the 38 days was the out-of-control driver who raced through a four-way stop. I actually noticed him coming and had not mounted the bike yet when he blasted through, so I didn't even count it as dangerous. My own worst move was entering the expressway by mistake in Oklahoma City. Nobody came close on that one either, but I was concerned that they might.

The fun stuff was never ending. Milkshakes were an old standby but my service as an unofficial Route 66 pie tester was new. Elvis' peanut butter, banana and chocolate pie at the Midpoint Café was the hands-down winner. Little Debbie peanut butter cakes were a staple this time. I remember on the cross-country ride how uncommon Little Debbie snacks were as I crossed the West. This time, they were everywhere. I know my hydration was better, but I ate nearly as much as during the 2013 cross-country ride. It was an incredible feeling to be hungry constantly. The large breakfasts, bought and consumed at night, hit the spot. I had fewer greasy things at night than before and the loss of a couple of pounds proved an extra boost. A little less of me to pedal up the hills was a good thing.

Despite losing those two pounds on the trip, I garnered a short list of favorite places to eat. Dairy Queen was my overall favorite, largely due to the best pineapple milkshakes I have ever discovered. They were always served with a smile and often with whipped cream at no charge. I even had two doubleheaders, or maybe they should have been called twin-killings. Those milkshakes never lasted long. Then came Denny's and those amazing blueberry pancakes and eggs, a slightly larger version of a similar order from IHOP. The Denny's in Normal took so much special care in giving me large servings of everything that I should have paid more, but they were happy to do it.

Another new favorite was Braum's, with the ice cream shop and great little fresh market grocery. Braum's should go national in my opinion. I stopped at McDonald's so often for bathroom, WiFi and food that it has to make the list.

Another constant was the long list of good motels. Every one of them had some special memory and most were very acceptable. I'm glad to have missed the almost $10 grilled cheese at the El Rancho, and I could have done without the price gouging at the Day's Inn in Chambers. Otherwise, I had no complaints and consider myself fortunate to escape the nighttime heat in comfortable motels along the way.

By addressing comfortable motels, I generally just consider the basics. Did the outlets and the lights work? Was the bed clean and firm? Was the motel located reasonably close to food sources? Did my budget like the price, and were there extra charges for a refrigerator or microwave? Was the ice machine close and working well? And last but probably most important after a long day, was my room quiet? I did like it if the TV was large and had plenty of channels.

But to be honest, I didn't watch TV much because there were other, more important demands on my time. Most evenings, I headed directly to get some food as soon as I was settled in. Sometimes, and especially if I knew that the motel was away from a grocery or other food choices, I stopped and loaded up my bags on the way. A few times, I actually had trouble keeping the food in the bags. The watermelon in Lebanon rode pretty well. Other demands that kept me away from concentrating on the TV were submitting my report to the paper, planning the next day and returning messages to those who followed the journey.

One more small thing — if I laid down on the bed, it was a safe bet that my eyes would close. I didn't worry much about the bed, but I did like good pillows and a working AC unit. It was a real plus to have it already cooling the room when I walked in. Nice folks running the places were an extra insight into the local area and enhanced my visit.

As a history nut, I was in heaven on this trip. All the Civil War sites and those places that Abraham Lincoln knew and loved were the highlights. The more recent history was special too, a lot of it about the motels and towns. Those 70-year-old motels visited by Reagan, Doris Day and all the movie stars were priceless overnights and I still feel a certain loss for not at least looking at Elvis' room at the Tradewinds.

Prior to the beginning of the journey, I read about all of the Route 66 attractions. Businesses would go out of the way to attract cars from the busy road. Nothing was better than the blue whale, for sure, and especially enjoyable were the giant men, the jackrabbit, the dinosaurs and the world's largest rocking chair. The Cadillac Ranch, the corner at Winslow, Mickey Mantle and Andy Payne, and probably Jesse James, too, were highlights never to be forgotten. I loved the character of the old bridges and truly hope they stay viable for many years to come.

Places that made the biggest impression were the Grand Canyon and the Painted Desert, so similar and just a few days apart. The Grand Canyon was just as good as advertised, just like last year's Niagara Falls. The Painted Desert was better than advertised and right up there with my all-time favorite, the Wind River Canyon in Wyoming.

Some places were missed. Most of them because I just didn't take the time to ride farther off the planned route. But had I taken the time, just a few more miles would probably have revealed something else worth seeing. That is the thing about this great country of ours. I mentioned Mickey Mantle and how I felt as if I spent part of the afternoon learning about the life of my boyhood hero. I never knew that Commerce was a part of this ride until just a few days before I pedaled into the town.

After the previous rides, I have picked my favorite states. On this ride, I enjoyed all of them and gave a slight edge to Arizona ahead of the others. Having the most miles of Route 66, the Grand Canyon and Williams helped Arizona eke out the best state award. My favorite towns were Williams, Arizona; Grants, New Mexico; New Buffalo, Indiana; and Pontiac, Illinois. Santa Monica and Chicago were just behind, getting extra credit as the start and finish of "America's Highway."

People, always foremost in my memories of the adventures, were incredible as always. Some were forgettable like the guy who lost his wallet and the driver who nearly lost his car. I never heard again from either one. The "manager" at the Day's Inn stands as the only listing in the jerk column especially after the Illinois state trooper realized how far I had ridden and became more personable.

Making real impressions were those who went out of their way to do something remarkable. Stephanie and Danielle, and their invitation to their church for breakfast, helped make the best day of the whole trip. Rasheed Hooda, on his own long journey now, continues at over 50 days of walking to Santa Monica. Nicholas, the very friendly cyclist in New Mexico, would have been someone worth riding with for a few days. And who could forget the Mayor of Golden who took time to flag me down as I passed by?

Others like Mac Bridges, Jack Connery and Doreen May influenced my trip by their continuous communication concerning areas that they knew well. Lauren Martz and I met for the first time nearly 2,000 miles from home and shared emails about how surprised her parents were to see their daughter in the paper. Amber Rose, the conductor on the Grand Canyon Railway, spent a day with me and made it especially enjoyable. I could go on and on about the people as they are truly the core of my enjoyment of these adventures.

Drivers were good to me, just as good as on the Underground Railroad ride from last summer. I got minimal horns and few negative verbal comments, less than I might have received had I spent the summer riding near home. What I did receive were constant waves and positive horns along the way. It was so cool to be riding along the interstate and receive a horn and long wave out the window of a truck or train as they passed by. I wonder how many of those drivers would want to trade seats, at least for a day. That might be a trade we could work out.

One driver who stood out, even though I don't know her name, was the lady in the van who stopped as I pedaled along the blistering uphill ride to Oatman. How did she know that I was close to being in trouble and running out of water? Somehow she did and made the perfect stop to see if I was OK and to offer me cold water. Her son, probably 10 years old, handed me the water out of the back of the van at the best possible time. I had forgotten how great a dripping-cold bottle of water could be at just the right time.

My equipment, now tried and true, was great again. I only camped once, in Romeroville, but that was more than anything because of the hot nights. The tent, sleeping bag and air mattress didn't get much use but they will be ready to go again. The panniers and handlebar bag, all slightly damaged in the 2014 Florida wreck, kept right on trucking. The tools all worked well. I don't like my helmet as much as I should, but it worked fine. My complete gear list seems to get smaller. New things were the roll-up water bottles and the wide-brimmed floppy hat, both suggestions from neighbors. They will ride with me again.

My erratic relationship with Adventure Cycling and their maps continued. They get great kudos for providing the maps that facilitate bike travel. What frustrates me is that the maps aren't updated often enough and the addendums that are sent along with the most recently printed maps are well behind too. At least two motels had been closed for 24 months but were still listed as available. An emailed suggestion of a better route received no response during my earlier rides. These are not big things but could be done better. Still, I already have my maps for next summer's adventure and know they will enhance the journey. I will definitely ask for the updated addendums before I leave.

One interesting story came to mind about my cyclometer, the bike's odometer. Just a couple of days after I started from Santa Monica, my cyclometer started displaying a low battery. I stopped and bought one at a Dollar General, but I didn't change it. I figured to change the battery when it quit. Then, just a few days later with the cyclometer still working, I couldn't find the battery. The next time I passed a Dollar General, I bought another one and kept it in the handlebar bag. The cyclometer still worked and about two weeks later, I found the one that I had bought on this trip and one that I had bought near the end of the first trip. I now had three batteries and was completely ready to change it out. When my Route 66 adventure came to an end in Walton, Indiana, I had three batteries and the cyclometer still worked.

The best day had to be the Sunday that I visited Commerce and Mickey Mantle's home. But the early stop to learn more about Andy Payne and then the encounter with Stephanie and Danielle got things rolling. The ending in Baxter Springs was nice, too. Finishing in a very close second was the amazing early morning ride with the animals out of Vega that led to miles of windmills flashing their red lights in sequence. All the while, I got to watch the spectacular flashes of the thunderstorm ahead as it gave way to the rainbow colors of the sunrise.

I am often asked to describe the worst day that I have had on the road. Simply, there are no bad days. Every single one of them is a thrilling adventure that is loaded with surprises. Others find it hard to understand how a blistering hot day of almost full-time exercise can be fun. I like the challenges and the endless hills and sometimes less-than-interesting scenery because it all adds to the experience. I want to be physically worn out at the end of the day, because then I have felt the bumps in the road, climbed the hills and fought the blustery winds as I experienced America.

Part of my good fortune over the years has been to just miss some truly horrendous disasters. Just after my ride was completed this year, thousands of residents were evacuated from San Bernardino because of forest fires. Damaged and destroyed were many homes and businesses along the streets I passed through. At least one Route 66 motel was destroyed, and a historic McDonald's with Route 66 décor was damaged seriously. I ate in that McDonald's. Santa Monica had extensive forest fires just days after I rode away. On other trips, I have missed by miles or days such issues as serious flooding, tornadoes and even a hurricane.

With my history of blood clot issues after these rides, I just had to beat the problem this time. I vowed to hydrate better than ever and to take an aspirin each day. On and on the miles went, and I just continued to feel stronger. My legs did great with the climbing, maybe the best ever. The great news is that I had scheduled a health assessment visit to Baptist Hospital in Winston-Salem for a few weeks after I returned home. There was no evidence of new clotting. The breathing issues that followed the other rides have not developed within the first two months following the ride's completion.

No real health issues have developed afterwards. During the ride, I took special precautions to wear the wide-brimmed hat and keep my face, and especially my ears, from burning in the bright desert sun. Burnt ears had been an issue before, but this time the hat did the job. I did get sunburned on the inside of both arms seriously by the end of the first week and had to wear a long sleeve shirt for most of the rest of the trip. They healed fine after about a week off the bike.

One more issue returned, just as it has for each of the long summer adventures. My toes gradually began to become numb over the course of the longer rides and especially after I was off the bike each day. Over the period of 38 days, many of them quite intense, the toes became almost permanently numb and tingly. But once again, as they have before, the toes returned to normal over about 60 days following the completion of the ride and return to normal activities.

What comes next? I certainly would be fine with getting right back on the bike tomorrow. In fact, more so than ever before, I can't wait to get back on the bike. Since returning home, I have realized that the easiest days are those that I spend riding across America. The other days, with all the responsibilities that come with being back in normal surroundings, are much harder. Give me the days on the bike any time!

At the completion of the Route 66 ride, I have now cycled in 39 states and visited four of the Great Lakes. Barring something unforeseen, I will head to the state of Washington during the summer of 2017 to add six more states with the part of the northern tier ride. My plans are to ride from west to east once again, my preferred direction, and add not only the state of Washington but those of North and South Dakota, Minnesota, Wisconsin and Iowa in hopes of bringing my total to 45. And across Wisconsin lies my chance to visit Lake Superior and complete all of the Great Lakes.

With that, my Route 66 adventure has truly come to an end. And just one more time, I can't wait to ride again.

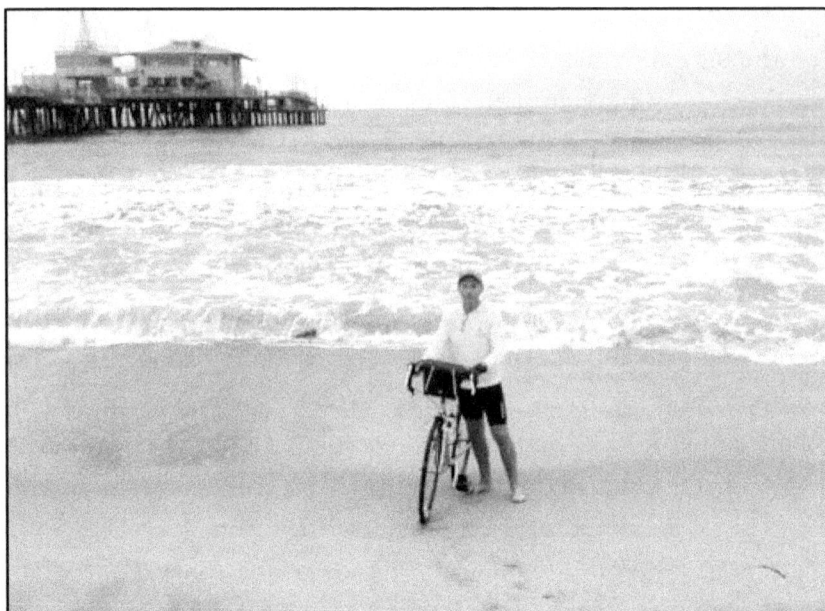

Rear wheel dipping on Santa Monica Beach.

Cynergy Cycles got my bike ready to go in Santa Monica, Calif.

All of the states along Route 66 allowed interstate riding except for Illinois.

The ride from Needles, Calif., to Oatman, Ariz., was oppressively hot, topping out at 114 degrees. Elevation gain was about 2,000 feet over four hours of riding.

185

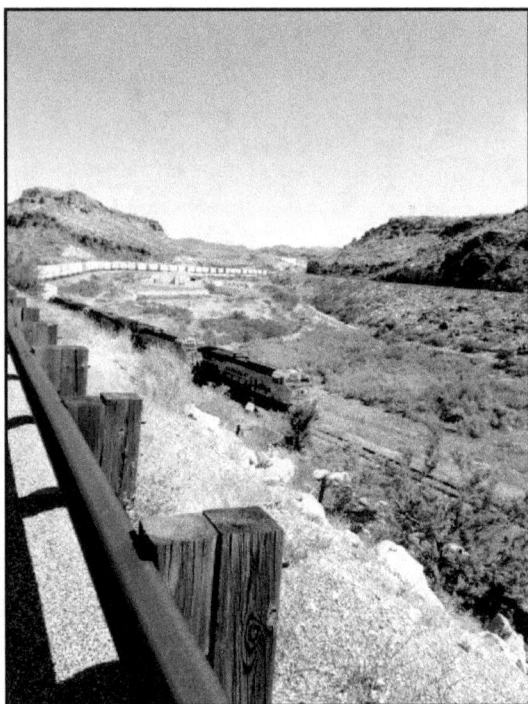

Trains were a constant over most of Route 66.

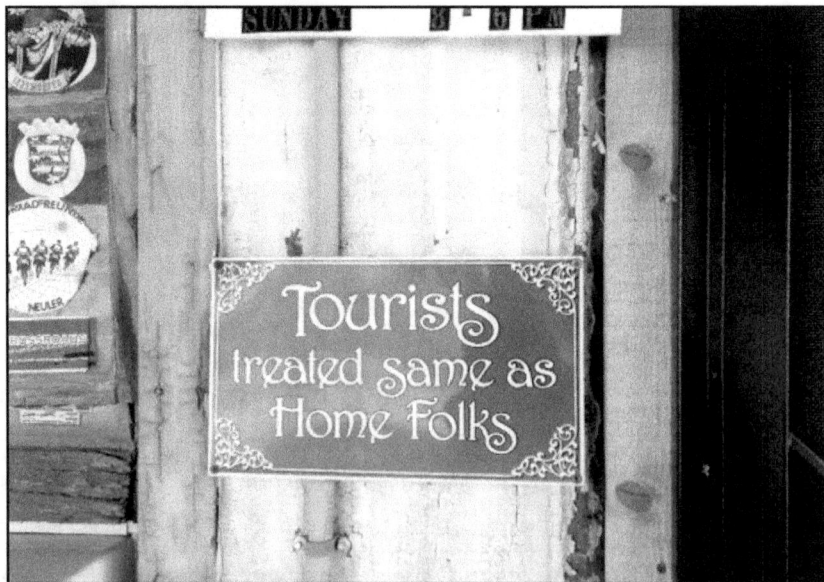

This was the theme all along Route 66.

186

The car didn't make it to Chicago, but I did.

The author at the Grand Canyon.

Train conductor Amber Rose on the Grand Canyon Railway from Williams, Ariz.

There was plenty of gunplay in Williams, Ariz., the author's favorite town along Route 66.

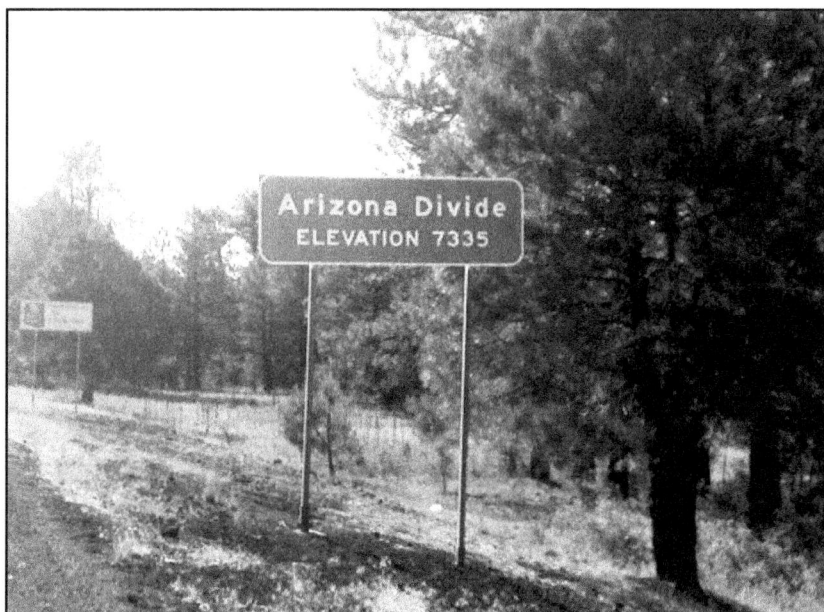

The highest point along Route 66.

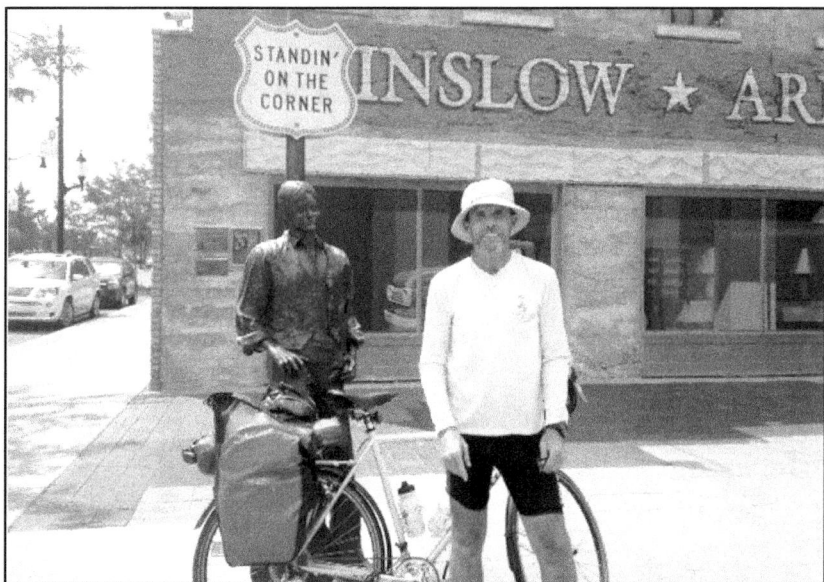

Standin' on the corner of Winslow, Ariz.

189

The mascot of the Jack Rabbit Trading Post near Joseph City, Ariz.

The St. Margaret Mary Mission in Paraje, N.M.

190

The Rio Grande River in Albuquerque, N.M.

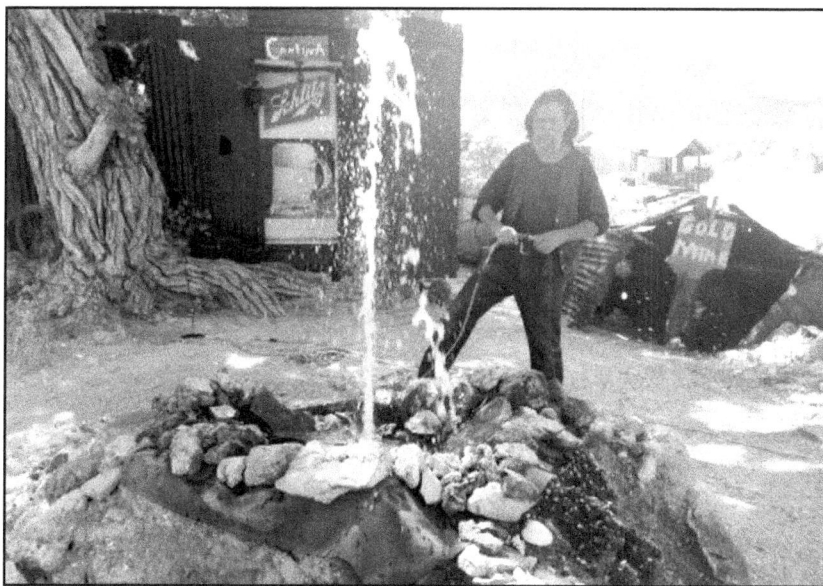

Mayor Leroy of Golden, N.M., demonstrates his roadside fountain.

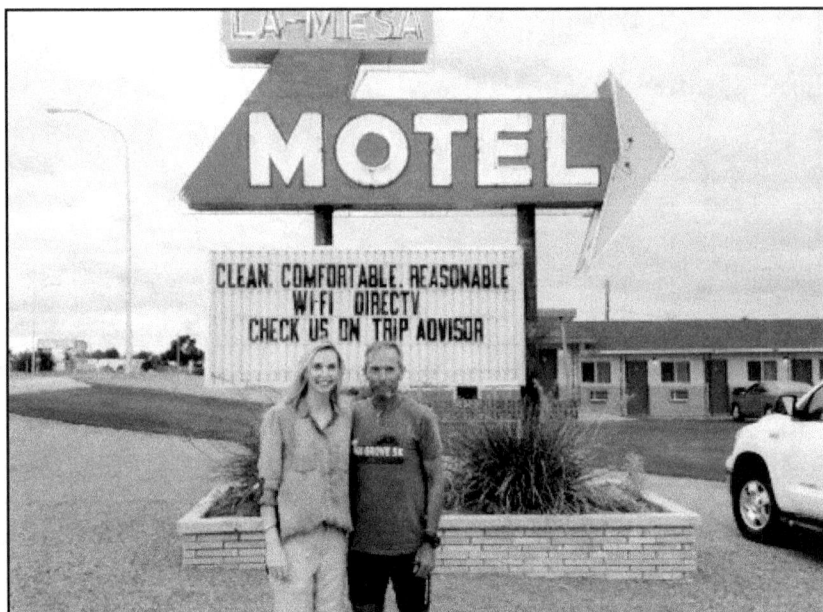

Lauren Martz from my hometown of Salisbury, N.C., found me in Santa Rosa, N.M.

The midpoint of Route 66, Adrian, Tex.

Cadillac Ranch, near Amarillo, Tex.

The most famous attraction on Route 66, the Blue Whale in Catoosa, Okla.

The winner
of the first
cross-country
foot race, Andy
Payne of Foyil,
Okla.

Mickey Mantle's boyhood home in Commerce, Okla.

194

Statue of New York Yankees great Mickey Mantle in Commerce, Okla., at his high school baseball field.

The last Rainbow Bridge on Route 66 is near Baxter, Kan.

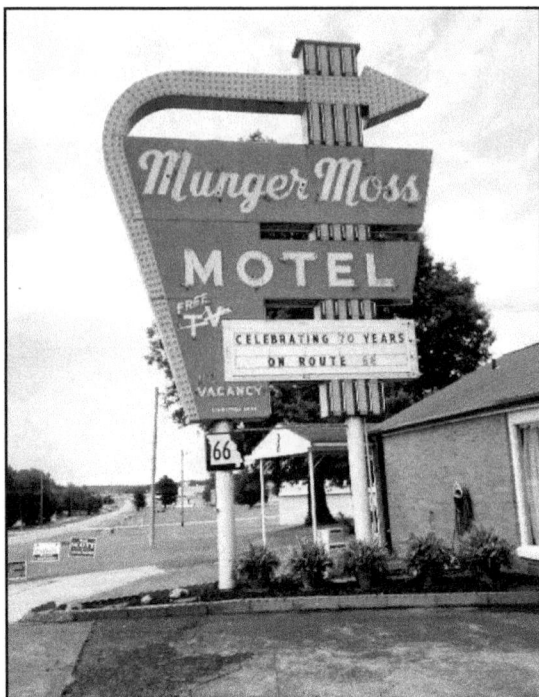

Just one of the oldest motels along Route 66, the Munger Moss Motel in Lebanon, Mo.

The Gateway Arch in St. Louis, Mo.

The Chain of Rocks Bridge across the Mississippi River near St. Louis is now a pedestrian bridge.

The Soulsby Shell Station in Mt. Olive, Ill., was built in 1926, one of dozens of historic stations along Route 66.

The only house that Abraham Lincoln ever owned, in Springfield, Ill.

One of the many Giant Men along Route 66, this is the Hot Dog Man in Atlanta, Ill.

The symbolic end of Route 66, the Buckingham Fountain in downtown Chicago.

The wheel dipping at the end of the water riding occurred in New Buffalo, Mich.

EPILOGUE

Even more than I expected

When I chose to journey from California to Chicago on Route 66, I thought that this ride could possibly be the best yet. I knew that the potential was there for a very entertaining ride, much the same as the "Mother Road" had entertained travelers for nearly a century. Yes, that's right, Route 66 did entertain travelers and getting there was truly about the journey. America's most celebrated highway got its start in the 1920s. On some parts of it, the scenery has not changed. Imagine riding for miles and seeing little that was different from what the automobile travelers could see out their windows during the glory days. Add to this my first ever encounter with the desert, and in the summer at that.

There were enough early ride hills that they kept me honest, and most of the rain that fell came as part of serious storms. The heat was an almost daily occurrence, and many readers seem amazed that bicycle riding was so much fun even with these conditions. Certainly, this ride had the most extreme and ongoing heat, and the desert winds were relentless most days. Thankfully, on only four days did I have a headwind. One of my favorite phrases remains, "Never waste a tailwind!"

The spectacular assets of mother nature included the Grand Canyon and the Painted Desert, while man-made attractions like the Blue Whale, Cadillac Ranch and the Giant Men always enhanced the journey. History lessons were around every turn, or more often at the end of a long stretch of Route 66 highway. The little towns like Williams, Pontiac and New Buffalo helped once again to shrink this great United States just a little bit more. Nearly every day, I get to say, "I know where that is. I rode through there!"

The special takeaways again are the people, but I won't attempt to list them here in fear of leaving someone out. My faith in Americans gets stronger on every ride! I receive such gifts repeatedly of just a smile or a helping hand, directions along with encouragement and especially those shared ideas to make the whole journey more fulfilling. More than ever before, I heard from readers all around the country who enjoyed sharing tips on the various areas as they rode along with me. It is my fervent endeavor not to bore people when I talk about the little towns or the people of my rides just because they have left a lasting impression on me.

Sensory experience is in no way out-of-fashion on the Mother Road. The smell of newly mown hay, the chugging sound of a train or the tolling of a church bell, the sight of so many murals and billboards or just the breeze on my face were all welcome and stimulating. I found it all amazing, often enhanced because it was so easy to pull over for longer exposure. Bike travel usually works this way, but Route 66 seemed to welcome it by saying, "Remember how travel used to be."

The question comes up almost daily: "Why?" My simple answer is, "Why not?" Only a few will choose to do something similar, but nothing compares with the excitement of rising each day, often too early, simply because I can't wait to get started. As I have said before, who else gets to experience anything close?

Speaking of simple, there is something else. Living life for more than a month with only the possessions that fit in two small bags on the back of a bike is not for everyone. But do we really need all the daily complications that go with having so many things? I think not, and relish the simple days of relying only on what I can easily carry on a bike. Surprisingly, the number of possessions lessens with each trip.

My quest for more cycled states continues and plans look good at this point for next summer's ride that would bring my total to 45 states and all five Great Lakes. Washington, North and South Dakota, Minnesota, Wisconsin and Iowa, plus Lake Superior, are on the horizon.

I can't close out any book without thanking God for my safety and continued health. Often readers mention my courage, but that courage comes directly from applying my own faith to daily situations. From day one in Astoria, Oregon, I began the practice of asking, "Lord, ride with me today!" No one rides alone when they ask for this assurance. *"Do not fear, for I am with you. Do not be afraid, for I am your God. I will strengthen you; I will help you; I will hold onto you with My righteous right hand."* — Isaiah 41:10.

In summary, my Route 66 ride was more than I expected and at this point rates as the most fun of my cycling adventures. Thanks once more for riding along, and let's plan to get together again soon!

www.ingramcontent.com/pod-product-compliance
Lightning Source LLC
LaVergne TN
LVHW051628080426
835511LV00016B/2228